D0058426

A Quiet Knowing

Gigi Graham Tchividjian

WITH

Ruth Bell Graham

W PUBLISHING GROUP™

www.wpublishinggroup.com

A Division of Thomas Nelson, Inc.
www.ThomasNelson.com

A QUIET KNOWING

Copyright © 2001, Ruth Bell Graham and Gigi Graham Tchividjian.

All rights reserved. No portion of this book may be reproduced, stored in a retrieval system, or transmitted in any form or by any means—electronic, mechanical, photocopy, recording, or other—except for brief quotations in printed reviews, without the prior permission of the publisher.

Published by W Publishing Group, a Division of Thomas Nelson, Inc., P.O. Box 141000, Nashville, Tennessee 37214.

Cover painting "Psalm 1" and tapestry by Kathy Hastings.
From the CD, "A Quiet Knowing—Canticles For The Heart"
by Jeff Johnson & Brian Dunning with John Fitzpatrick (AKD-1504)
www.arkmusic.com ©2000 D&K Studios/Ark Records, Inc.

Information concerning *A Quiet Knowing,* the book, music CD, video, conference curriculum, conferences, and concerts, as well as other books by Gigi Graham Tchividjian and Ruth Bell Graham can be found at the following internet address:

www.quietknowing.com

Unless otherwise indicated, Scripture quotations used in this book are from The Holy Bible, New International Version, copyright © 1973, 1978, 1984, International Bible Society. Used by permission of Zondervan Bible Publishers. Other Scripture quotations are from the following sources: The King James Version of the Bible (KJV). The New King James Version (NKJV), copyright © 1979, 1980, 1982, Thomas Nelson, Inc., Publishers. The Amplified New Testament (AMP), copyright © 1954, 1958, The Lockman Foundation. All rights reserved.

Book jacket design by Patton Brothers Design, San Diego, CA (www.pattonbros.com)

Library of Congress Cataloging-in-Publication Data applied for.
ISBN 0-8499-1676-3

Printed in the United States of America

01 02 03 04 05 06 QWK 6 5 4 3 2 1

CONTENTS

The fruit of righteousness will be peace;
the effect of righteousness will be
quietness and confidence forever.

—Isaiah 32:17

INTRODUCTION

A Quiet Knowing

Scripture tells us, in the words of Isaiah, that "the fruit of righteousness will be peace; the effect of righteousness will be quietness and confidence forever" (32:17). With our self-reliance deeply shaken by the events of September 11, 2001, that "confidence forever" is what I refer to as a quiet knowing. It's the deep knowledge inside that you have a personal relationship with Jesus Christ. And nurturing this relationship gives us a peace that "passeth all understanding" (Phil. 4:7 KJV).

A quiet knowing is also a sense of serenity. Most people I know are desperately searching for a sense of serenity. Serenity is that inner peace that comes with the certainties of knowing in whom you believe, what you believe, who you are, and where you're going.

It was said of Mother Teresa that she was blessed with certainties. I think that could also be said of my mother, Ruth Bell Graham. She is certain of who she is because she is certain of the One who loves her, the One in Whom she has put her faith. She's been able to pass that certainty on to her children. And I, as her eldest, am so grateful that she passed that certainty on to me.

Recently, Mother and I were sitting in her bedroom, she in her "ledge of quiet" (a comfortable overstuffed chair by the bay window) and I in the wingback chair beside the open fire, discussing the meaning of this little phrase, "a quiet knowing," taken from one of her poems.

We agreed that for us, "a quiet knowing" is, as the old hymn says, the "blessed assurance, [that] Jesus is mine." It is knowing that all is well between God and me, that "all is well with my soul."

The Greek word translated "peace" in the New Testament is a much more complex and comprehensive word than the one we use. It does not mean simply absence of trouble, but total well-being. It includes everything (all the ingredients, the experiences, and the pieces that God allows into our lives) that makes for our highest good.[1] A quiet knowing is what we experience when we are aware of this fact.

Through the years, Mother has shared many of her own personal struggles, doubts, and cares with her pen through her poetry. The title *A Quiet Knowing* is taken from the following poem:

Sunk in this gray
depression
I cannot pray.
How can I give
expression
when there're no words
to say?
This mass of vague
foreboding
of aching care,

fear with its
overloading
short-circuits prayer.
Then in this fog
of tiredness,
this nothingness I find
a quiet knowing
that He is kind.

—RUTH BELL GRAHAM

"A quiet knowing" comes through a personal relationship and deep intimacy with God through Jesus Christ. It is the confidence that we have in Him that He is in all and above all, that everything He does and allows in our lives is for our good and for His glory. It is being always and forever conscious of His encircling presence.

We trust that as you share with us the following pages, you will begin to acquaint yourself with Him in a very personal way and that you will experience a new level of intimacy with Him so that you, too, can participate in the certainties of *A Quiet Knowing*.

Where is God my Maker,
who gives songs in the night?
—Job 35:10

Lo, the very hairs He numbers,

And no daily care encumbers,

Them that share His every blessing,

And His help in woes distressing.

Children of the Heavenly Father

Chapter 1

DEALING WITH DAILY CARES

As a small child, I often went into Mother's room at night, where I would find her still up reading her Bible or maybe on her knees praying. However, I'm sure there were many nights when she could cry out with Job, "Where is God my Maker, who gives songs in the night?" (35:10).

Mother was alone much of the time. And although she knew that it was worth the price because what Daddy was doing was important from eternity's perspective, it didn't alleviate the pain of loneliness. In fact, she said she would often get one of Daddy's jackets out of the closet and sleep with it when her loneliness became too much.

Mother has always believed in the all-sufficiency of God. And she has always relied on the authority and encouragement of Scripture to help her through her days and nights. Mother found, in Christ, the strength and sufficiency she needed to get through the dark and lonely nights as well as the difficult days as a "single mom." She has experienced firsthand what the old hymn says, that our Lord "no daily care encumbers them that share His every blessing and His help in woes distressing." This unswerving trust in the goodness and sufficiency of God she has passed on to each of her children.

We all experience difficult times—times when the ache of loneliness just won't go away, when sadness overwhelms us, or when anxious thoughts keep us awake long into the night. It was probably on such a night that Mother penned the following words:

"Give me your nights,"
the quiet voice
of God said to my
pressured heart.
Wakeful and fretting
I knew I had the
choice:
For me the easy or
the better part?

Nights are for sleeping,
one of His kindest gifts
Which, if He withholds
is for a special reason,

Some work the daylight
some the midnight shift
Could nights become
for me a special season?

"Give me your nights";
His voice unheard
spoke again. And my heart
sleepless, stirred,
listened in silence
then acquiesced.
For only in compliance
I am blessed.

—RUTH BELL GRAHAM

I was sitting with a group of friends one day, when one of them looked up at me and commented, "Well, you certainly have it all together." I couldn't have been more taken aback, because I have always considered myself a struggler. Nothing comes easy for me, especially being good or "having it all together." As a child, I remember waking each morning to the sound of singing birds and chirping katydids, longing and hoping with all that was in me that I would be good that day. Before my feet ever touched the floor, I pleaded with the Lord to help me not to blow it. I prayed that this would be the day that He and I would get it together.

Sometimes I made it through breakfast. But often I wouldn't even make it that far. I'd pick an argument, lose my temper, say the wrong thing, or talk too much. Then, as Mother described, "that sick feeling in the pit of your stomach, [which] says that you have blown it again" would rush over me. Utterly discouraged, I would write the day off as a lost cause.

Mother says of me, "There never was a little girl who tried harder to be good but was so bad at it." I was a good little repenter, however (with so much practice), and I discovered early that failure isn't final. So, the next day, I was ready to try again. However, as the months turned into years and this pattern continued, I became more and more discouraged.

It seemed that, for me at least, living the Christian life was one gigantic effort. I read how the Lord loved "a gentle and quiet spirit" (1 Pet. 3:4), and since this did anything but describe me, I couldn't see how I was ever going to please Him. (It was years before I realized that this verse does not describe our personalities, but our attitudes of submission toward Him.) I looked with envy upon those who seemed to be Christlike without struggling so hard. Reading about the fruit of the Spirit in Galatians 5:22–23, I would examine my life and find little evidence of patience, longsuffering, or gentleness.

I fell so far short of all that I thought was Christlike that I began to wonder if Jesus lived in me at all. Yet, I knew I had given Him my life when I was four and had reaffirmed this many times. Even so, when I listened to sermons about how the Lord changes our lives and makes us new creations, I sometimes wished I had never accepted Christ into my life so that I could start all over and become "really" converted. Maybe then I would see the dramatic change in my life for which I so longed. On one such day when I was struggling with these things, I wrote the following poem:

I read verse after verse,

I find

I am supposed to have

Rest,

Peace,

Gentleness,

Quietness of heart

    and mind.

I don't.

I pray,

thoughts stray

every which way.

I cannot even say

how I really feel.

If I try,

it comes out wrong.

Oh, how I long

to be

what I am not.

—GIGI GRAHAM TCHIVIDJIAN

I remember one day, as a young mother, sitting in our home in Switzerland and reading one of those beautifully written books that describe the kind of Christian life I longed to live. After a while, I put the book down. As I looked out through the window, over the flower-strewn fields and beyond to the blue alpine lake framed by snow-covered mountains, tears began streaming down my face, and in utter frustration, I cried aloud, "But HOW? How? How do I do it?"

Years have gone by since that day in Switzerland. Many more tears of frustration have found their way down my cheeks, and that was not the last time I have cried out, "But HOW?" However, I have learned many things since that day, and I am so grateful I never gave up in total despair. The Christian life is not about having it all together; it is a commitment to a process.

Growing up in a Christian home and in a small community inhabited mostly by retired missionaries and pastors, I was surrounded all through my childhood by beautiful examples of mature, full-grown, fragrant Christians. They had all been walking life's road hand in hand with their Lord for many years. Then I attended a Christian boarding school, where I was required to read many of the classics of godly men and women who never seemed to struggle in their Christian walks. So I thought the word *Christian* was synonymous with godly, Christ-like, mature, wise, gentle, and perfect. I compared myself to these saints, failing to realize that their mature faith had taken many years of growing, learning, trusting, submitting, abiding, obeying, and much practice. Since I was not (and still am not) a very patient person, I was extremely impatient with myself. I simply couldn't understand why it was taking me so long to mature spiritually. I once heard a pastor say, "You are young only once, but you can be immature for a lifetime." I was sure this was to be my lot in life.

Sometimes I didn't even feel converted. How could my acceptance of Christ when I was four years old be for real? I looked at all the things I had done and just didn't feel saved. I would become so discouraged in my Christian walk. It took me some time to learn that our feelings are often Satan's counterfeit for faith.

It somehow escaped me, as a young Christian, that these dear saints had been walking with, working for, and getting to know their Lord for many years. It didn't occur to me that they, too, had struggled, some for many long, hard years. They had not been born full-grown or in full bloom. They had learned many lessons and had been taught much from their spiritual bumps and scrapes and skinned knees.

I remember once, as my two-year-old son was running to me, he tripped over himself and fell. He hopped up and said, "Oops, I dropped myself." He didn't get discouraged in his efforts to walk; he accepted this as par for the course for someone of his age. He didn't compare himself to me, but on occasion, he did ask me to help him along.

Each time I "dropped myself" spiritually, the devil left his calling card of discouragement. I was measuring my spiritual growth and progress by the beautiful Christian role models around me. I was becoming more and more despondent because I couldn't measure up, instead of simply accepting and acknowledging my limitations, as my little son had done, and asking for His help, which He would have lovingly and readily given.

I began to wake up to the realization that if I continued to try to live victoriously in my own strength, I could expect nothing but failure and discouragement. I began to see that I was expecting perfection. I was expecting more of myself than the Lord was expecting of me! I was trying to win the battles alone and was disappointed with myself when I lost. But the Lord doesn't expect us to fight alone. He says that He will go with us and fight for us. "For the battle is not yours, but God's. . . . You will not have to fight this battle. Take up your positions; stand firm and see the deliverance the LORD will give you" (2 Chron. 20:15, 17).

When I finally began to realize and accept this, an incredible thing happened to me. I began to relax! Now when I fail (as I continue to do), I try to be like the seventeenth-century monk Brother Lawrence, who was very sensible of his faults and not discouraged by them. He confessed them to God, and when he had done so, he peacefully resumed his life.

I had read that, as a Christian, I should be as the butterfly, which flies high above the ground it once crawled upon as a caterpillar. Instead of realizing spiritual maturity was a long-term goal, I had become downhearted in my caterpillar state and had looked with envy on all the beautiful, high-flying spiritual butterflies around me.

But as I observed these spiritual butterflies, I noticed they were not concerned about being saints at all. In fact, they were not even conscious of the fact that they were saints. Instead, they were deeply conscious of their need for total dependency upon the Lord. They were much more concerned about their personal relationships and walks with the Lord than about their spiritual perfection or their usefulness to Him. They were so totally one with Him that all they did became a service to Him, whether it was washing dishes, caring for others, or leading a Bible study. They did not spend time wondering if they had the Lord; they just made sure that He had them.

We have the promise that "he who began a good work in you will carry it on to completion until the day of Christ Jesus" (Phil. 1:6). In Psalm 138:8 we read, "The

LORD will fulfill his purpose for me." He loves us too much to quit now. He has a personal interest in making sure that one day we "mount up with wings" (Isa. 40:31 KJV).

One winter, in our home near Milwaukee, Wisconsin, I was reading in my bedroom when I happened to glance out the window at our big oak tree, which was in the middle of our circular driveway. All of the leaves had fallen, but up in the top of its branches I saw a big bunch of ugly, brown leaves. I didn't think that they looked very nice, but I didn't see how I was going to be able to climb up there and pull them off. So I went back to reading.

A few months later, I was sitting by that same window and noticed that the big bunch of brown leaves in the old oak were gone and that in their place were new, bright green leaves. I hadn't even noticed, but as the new life of spring began to flow through the tree and the new leaves began to sprout, the brown leaves just fell off all by themselves.

So it is in the Christian life. As we abide in Christ

through prayer and Bible study and allow the sap of the Holy Spirit to flow through us, then our old habits, actions, and desires just fall off and are replaced by the fruit of the Spirit.

It is His completeness that makes up for our incompleteness, His perfection that covers our imperfections. "And ye are complete in him" (Col. 2:10 KJV). He is perfect, and until we see Him face to face, we will never be perfect. But must remain committed to the process. Amy Carmichael once told of watching a goldsmith in India who was refining gold. He patiently sat beside the pot, in a small cubicle. She asked the goldsmith, "When do you know when it is purified?" He replied, "When I see my reflection in it."

I failed to realize that the pure-as-gold saints I grew up around had been through much refining. What I was observing was the reflection of the Master Goldsmith, after years of careful purifying. And so it will be with us as we walk with the Lord, allowing Him to refine us.

Elizabeth Strachen, a friend of my mother's, once shared these thoughts with my mother:

God loves and forgives me and accepts me, just the way I am, unconditionally. And He will love me into perfection. Because He loves and forgives and accepts me as I am, then I love (in the right way) and accept myself just the way I am—in the body He has given me, with my limitations and imperfections—because He can use them as a showcase for His grace and glory.

One of the greatest trials and miseries many Christians struggle with is our seeming inability to accept ourselves as the Lord has accepted us. Like me, perhaps you have tried so hard and failed so often that you are frequently discouraged. At times like these, we need to remember to be grateful for the patience of the Master Goldsmith, even with this poor metal. And remember, any old piece of tin can reflect if it is clean.

Again, it's grace . . . His grace.

CHILDREN OF THE HEAVENLY FATHER

Children of the heav'nly Father
Safely in His bosom gather;
Nestling bird nor star in heaven
Such a refuge e'er was given.

God His own doth tend and nourish;
In His holy courts they flourish.
From all evil things He spares them;
In His mighty arms He bears them.

Neither life nor death shall ever
From the Lord His children sever;
Unto them His grace He showeth,
And their sorrows all He knoweth.

Though He giveth or He taketh,
God His children ne'er forsaketh;
His the loving purpose solely
To preserve them pure and holy.

WORDS: CAROLINE V. SANDELL-BERG, 1832–1903;
TR. ERNST W. OLSON, 1870–1958

Submit to God and be at peace with him;
in this way prosperity will come to you.
—JOB 22:21

Be Thou my vision,

oh Lord of my heart

Nought be all else to me,

save that Thou art

Thou my best thought

by day or by night

Waking or sleeping,

Thy presence my light.

Chapter 2

Be Thou My Vision

HELP FOR DIFFICULT DAYS AND SLEEPLESS NIGHTS

PART 1 *Prayer*

As a young girl, I knew Mother was deeply and intensely committed to Jesus Christ. With Daddy gone much of time, we knew that Mother relied on her personal relationship with the Lord to help her day by day.

However, as in all of our lives, there have been times when Mother experienced a certain foreboding, loneliness, depression, or discouragement. When we were young, she didn't share these times with us children. As I have often said, she gave us the times of sunshine; the others she shared with the Lord and her pen often late at night:

Into the heart of the Infinite can a mere mortal
        hope to gain access,
what with no part of me geared to His greatness,
to His vastness my infinite less?
Yet the longing for Him was so wide and so deep,
by day it crowded life's thronging,
by night it invaded my sleep

Then came the pain:
again . . .
        and again . . .
                and again . . .

As if a wing tip were brushing the tears from my face
for the breath of a second I knew the unknowable,
glimpsed invisible grace.

And I lay where for long in despair I had lain;
entered, unshod, the holy There where God
        dwells with His pain—
alone with the pain of the price He had paid
in giving His Son for a world gone astray
—the world He had made.

My heart lay in silence,
worshipped in silence;
and questioned no more.

—RUTH BELL GRAHAM

Many times I have been at my wits' end about something, desperately tired, or so discouraged that I felt more like giving up than trying. I have fallen on my knees beside my bed or poured out my heart to the Lord while driving the car or doing the laundry, sometimes without a word, knowing, as Spurgeon once said, "Groanings which cannot be uttered are often prayers which cannot be refused."

What is prayer? What do we mean when we say that we pray? Some teaching on prayer makes it seem too vague, mystical, spiritual, or even too difficult for us simple, busy women. However, prayer is practical.

Others imagine that prayer is kneeling with closed eyes and speaking in eloquent phrases. This is perhaps one kind of prayer, but I believe prayer is communication with the One who loves us most, the One who cares for us and cherishes us more than anyone else, the One who always has our best interest in His heart and mind. Prayer is an attitude of worship and thanksgiving. And this can be done in any position—standing, sitting, kneeling, or lying down. It can be done any time of day or night—as the old hymn says, "Waking or sleeping, Thy presence my light." We can pray while driving, working, cleaning, playing, waking up to face our day, or when we can't sleep at night. The apostle Paul tells us to "pray without ceasing" (1 Thess. 5:17 KJV). For me, more often then not, this means that I pray without ceasing my work. I just talk to the Lord as I carry on my responsibilities.

Prayer is a vital part of every person's spiritual experience. We are all aware of how important verbal communication is to any relationship, such as with our spouses, friends, or coworkers. A quick way to destroy a relationship is to avoid talking. Likewise, prayer is simply verbal communication with God. This simple principle was beautifully exemplified by a dear, older friend who passed away recently. He always started his prayers with, "And Lord . . ." In other words, he was just continuing where he had left off with his last conversation with God.

Prayer is also the way we get to know God. We pray in order to receive a better understanding of God. Prayer is one of the important elements of nourishing our personal relationships with God. I have discovered that the

more time I spend in prayer, the better I begin to know God Himself and the more I see things from His perspective. This in turn brings the needed transformation in my disposition and attitude, which gives me more strength and serenity.

Prayer doesn't so often change the outward circumstances or our situations as much as it transforms the way we view those circumstances and situations. Often it is our spirits and our attitudes that need changing.

At one point in the journeys of the Israelites, they began to circle around a certain mountain. They continued in this manner for many days, until the Lord came

and told them, "Ye have compassed this mountain long enough: turn you northward" (Deut. 2:3 KJV). So it is with me. I circle whatever my particular mountain is—discouragement, disappointment, busyness, frustration, or worry—and soon the Lord has to say, "Gigi, you have been going around in circles over this matter long enough." More often than not, it is in prayer that He speaks to me in this way. It is in prayer that I realize my attitude needs to change and my spirit needs to be turned around.

Not only do we speak to God in prayer, but He also speaks to our hearts. I remember as a young girl, hearing mother softly singing:

Speak, Lord, in the stillness,
While I wait on Thee,
Hush my heart to listen
In expectancy.

Some of you may be wondering why we need to pray, especially if God knows everything anyway. One reason is that prayer develops our spiritual relationships and intimacy with God. And another reason is simply that we are told in Scripture to pray, and we do so out of obedience.

If we wish to be obedient, then we have no choice but to pray. Prayer does not come easily for me, especially public prayer. When I was a young girl, I went to a very strict boarding school. Because my father was a well-known preacher, much was expected of me even though I was only twelve years old. One night I was summoned to the headmistress, who was a large, tall, very intimidating woman. She took me into her room and criticized my prayers. She told me that my prayers were not mature enough, that I didn't quote enough Scripture when I prayed. From then on, I have always been a little intimidated praying in front of others.

It is easy to find excuses not to pray. We are too busy, don't have time, don't know how, don't feel like it, etc. But if we find ourselves too busy to do what we have been told to do, then it stands to reason we are doing some things that we were not told to do. And if I pray without ceasing my work, then I don't have an excuse. The best way to learn to pray is to pray.

I have discovered that I will seldom pray if I always wait until I feel like it. When I feel the least like praying is when I find I need prayer the most. Many only pray when things go wrong, when there is a crisis or disturbance in their lives. They use prayer as a last resort. While I am sure that God hears these prayers also, prayer is not something we do just because we are desperate. It is something we do because we want to communicate with the One who loves us. It is something He has asked us to do in order for us to develop a relationship with Him. He longs for . . . awaits our communication with Him.

However, there is a side to prayer that requires discipline. Most of us are willing to work at whatever we value—a relationship, sport, hobby, etc. If we value prayer, we should be willing to set aside the time and energy required to pray on a consistent basis. After all, Jesus Himself felt the necessity to pray. If He needed prayer for strength and refreshment, how much more do we need it!

We can make prayer both practical and workable. I
want to share a couple of simple tools that someone gave
me years ago for starting on this exciting journey.

P	Praise
R	Repentance
A	Asking
Y	Yourself

Put another way

A	Adoration
C	Confession
T	Thankfulness
S	Supplication

Praise/Adoration. Prayer is not a heavenly shopping list. It is not simply asking God for things we want. Prayer is acknowledging Who God is and what He has done for us. A good way to do this is with an open Bible. We can also praise Him as we enjoy an early morning walk, singing, "When morning guilds the skies, my heart awakening cries, 'May Jesus Christ be praised." Simply saying "thank You" to God can also be a form of praise.

Repentance/Confession. Scripture tells us that "if we confess our sins, he is faithful and just to forgive us our sins" (1 John 1:9 KJV). When we as believers sin, our positions in Christ remain sure but our relationships are hindered, just like when our children disobey or do something to displease us. They are still our children, but until they confess and apologize, our relationships with them are strained. However, if we as Christians continue in sin without confession and repentance, it will not be long before we cease to have any fellowship with the Lord.

Public confession should be general, but private confession needs to be specific, not just, "Forgive our many sins." He takes our sins and removes them as far as the east is from the west. He buries them in the deepest sea, and as Corrie Ten Boom used to say, He puts up a sign: "No Fishing Allowed." Once we have confessed and repented of our sins, then we can be assured of His forgiveness and the complete restoration of the relationship.

Asking/Supplication. God tells us to ask. "Ask and it will be given to you; seek and you will find" (Matt. 7:7). While I was in boarding school, I discovered that nothing was too big for Him to handle and nothing too small for Him to care about. I went to Him for everything, and He became my very best friend. We can go to the Lord as often as we please without any fear of being a bother. There is no call waiting and no voice mail. We can go to Him for anything and everything.

In some mysterious way God has chosen to limit His working here on earth in cooperation with our prayers. I don't understand this, but it is true. And it elevates prayer to a place of utmost importance so that we often find that prayer is a spiritual battle. Satan tries His best to distract and discourage us. He would like nothing better than for us to fail to pray.

My prayer life has always been rather informal. I have often been encouraged by the writings of George MacDonald, who said, "Never wait for a fitter time or place to talk to Him. He will listen as thou walkest."[1] Prayer for me is a way of life. As Oswald Chambers once described prayer: "It is the life. It is for the believer, like breathing. . . . We are not conscious of it but it is going on."[2]

Brother Lawrence said that he had a sense of God's presence by continually conversing with Him. He said that he always talked to God with the greatest simplicity, speaking plainly and frankly. So it is with me. I humbly but boldly approach Almighty God and speak with Him as to my very closest friend. What an awesome privilege!

Prayer is both the way in and the way out. It is the way into Him, the way into knowing His heart, the way

into abiding in His love. It is also the way out of frustration, discouragement, anxiety, burdens, and all that causes heaviness. The Scriptures tell us, "Acquaint now thyself with him [become more and more intimate with God], and be at peace" (Job 22:21 KJV). I believe that certainties, serenity, that "quiet knowing," come in proportion to our intimacy with Him.

If we want to experience a quiet knowing, then we have to converse regularly with our heavenly Father. We must maintain an open channel, a constant attitude of prayer, and also read and study God's Word, because the effectiveness of our prayer lives is hinged on our depth and knowledge of Scripture.

BE THOU MY VISION

Be Thou my vision, O Lord of my heart;
Naught be all else to me, save that Thou art
Thou my best thought, by day or by night,
Waking or sleeping, Thy presence my light.

Be Thou my Wisdom, and Thou my true Word;
I ever with Thee and Thou with me, Lord;
Thou my great Father, I Thy true son;
Thou in me dwelling, and I with Thee one.

Be Thou my battle-shield, sword for my fight,
Be Thou my dignity, Thou my delight.
Thou my soul's shelter, Thou my high tower.
Raise Thou me heavenward, O Power of my power.

Riches I heed not, nor man's empty praise,
Thou mine inheritance, now and always:
Thou and Thou only, first in my heart,
High King of heaven, my Treasure Thou art.

High King of heaven, my victory won,
May I reach heaven's joys, O bright heav'ns Son!
Heart of my own heart, whatever befall,
Still be my vision, O ruler of all.

WORDS: ANCIENT IRISH, TR. MARY BYRNE, 1880–1931;
VERSIFIED, ELEANOR H. HULL, 1860–1935

But his delight is in the law of the LORD,
and on his law he meditates day and night.

—Psalm 1:2

Be Thou my vision,

oh Lord of my heart

Nought be all else to me,

save that Thou art

Thou my best thought

by day or by night

Waking or sleeping,

Thy presence my light.

Be Thou My Vision

Chapter 3

HELP FOR DIFFICULT DAYS AND SLEEPLESS NIGHTS

PART 2 *Scripture*

A few years ago, my husband, Stephan, and I spent some time living in Israel. The church we attended also celebrated Sabbath (Saturday worship), and often after church we would take a drive away from the city of Jerusalem and into the surrounding hills. These hills are often barren and rocky, and to venture too far off the main highway is to quickly find yourself in hot, dry, forsaken areas where few ever venture. As far as the eye can see there is nothing but sand, rocks, steep cliffs, deep ravines, and hills, hills, and more hills, where shadows play eerie games of hide-and-seek. Occasionally, a lone bird circles overhead, suddenly swooping down to catch unsuspecting prey. On one such afternoon, I was gazing out over these hills when my eye caught sight of what I thought was something green. I was curious about the strange growth in the middle of all that barrenness. Then I was told that, unseen to me, there was a little underground stream flowing down the side of that hill, and on both sides of that little stream was lush, green growth.

Each time I remember that little afternoon outing, I am reminded of the man in Psalm 1:2–3 who delighted in and meditated upon the teachings of God. It was said of him that he "is like a tree planted by streams of water, which yields its fruit in season and whose leaf does not wither. Whatever he does prospers" (v. 3).

God delights in leading us "beside quiet waters" (Ps. 23:2), waters that provide refreshment. From the Garden of Eden to the throne room of heaven, God promises provision for refreshment, rivers of living water that refresh our souls and spirits (see Gen. 2:10 and Rev. 7:17).

Abiding in Him and His Word provides refreshment for the parched, strength for the weary, encouragement for the discouraged, food for hungry souls, light for those who have lost their way, a quenching for the spiritually thirsty, and a quiet knowing that He is in control.

On days when I am spiritually dry, I read, "The LORD will . . . satisfy your needs in a sun-scorched land. . . . You will be like a well-watered garden, like a spring whose waters never fail" (Isa. 58:11).

When I need strength, I find, "He gives strength to the weary and increases the power of the weak" (Isa. 40:29).

When I worry or become anxious about the future, He assures me, "I will go before you and will level the mountains; I will break down gates of bronze and cut through bars of iron" (Isa. 45:2).

When I am facing problems too great for me, I read, "The LORD is good, a refuge in times of trouble. He cares for those who trust in him" (Nahum 1:7).

When I am discouraged or depressed, I am reminded

through the words of Isaiah that He has given me a way out if I will put on "a garment of praise instead of a spirit of despair" (Isa. 61:3).

When I start to think of myself, He reminds me in Mark 10:45 that He "did not come to be served, but to serve, and to give his life as a ransom for many."

When I tend to get fussy, I turn to Proverbs 21:9 and am quickly brought back to reality when I read, "[It is] better to live on a corner of the roof than share a house with a quarrelsome wife."

When I worry about our children, I am reminded that they are His and that, if I am faithful, then He promises, "All thy children *shall be* taught of the LORD; and great *shall be* the peace of thy children" (Isa. 54:13 KJV).

There is a promise, an exhortation, a direction, a comfort, or an encouragement for every situation, every problem, and every need we will ever experience.

Just before the birth of my sixth child, I suddenly developed an unfounded fear of the delivery and birth. I was tired, and the thought of the delivery and the pain frightened me. I prayed about this fear, asking the Lord for His comfort and strength. I turned to the Scriptures and read Isaiah 46:4, in which the Lord promises, "I have made, and I will bear; even I will carry, and will deliver *you*" (KJV). A sense of peace flooded me and I meditated on this verse often during the delivery and the birth of my daughter. Just as King Solomon observed many years ago, and I have experienced time and again, "not one word has failed of all [God's] good promises" (1 Kings 8:56). His promises prove true, and His strength is sufficient.

The wife of Jonathan Goforth, a missionary to China many years ago, had a large family, including many small children to care for. She was also responsible for much of the mission work. Once, when she was overburdened and finding her strength insufficient, she decided to search the Scriptures to see if there were any conditions for receiving His strength. She says: "The result of my study was a surprise and joy to me, and later a blessing and help to many to whom I later passed it on, because, every condition laid forth, the very weakest could fulfill."[1]

CONDITIONS FOR RECEIVING STRENGTH

Weakness: 2 Corinthians 12:9–10

No Might: Isaiah 40:29

Sitting Still: Isaiah 30:2

Waiting on God: Isaiah 40:31

Quietness: Isaiah 30:15

Confidence: Isaiah 30:15

Joy in the Lord: Nehemiah 8:10

Poor: Isaiah 25:4

Needy: Isaiah 25:4

Abiding in Christ: Philippians 4:13

Scripture is not only necessary for our strength and encouragement, but also gives us a light for our paths. We find leading and direction for our lives within its pages, principles, and precepts. Scripture is the Manufacturer's instruction book. Have you ever purchased a lovely sweater only to wash it without first checking the manufacturer's instructions? I have. And yes, I ruined it. But I couldn't blame the manufacturer.

Scripture is also our reference point. A few years ago, the highway department was repainting the lines of the interstate near where we live. For a few days on just a short section of this highway there were no lines. As a consequence, there were many accidents because there were no reference points.

One evening when the children were younger, we were all sitting around the dinner table when I noticed that our eldest seemed a bit discouraged. He had been having a hard time being good, especially in school. I tried to help by suggesting that he might be encouraged by remembering some of the Bible verses he had memorized.

This seemed to get him even more discouraged. He said what he needed was "a cap with all the verses he knew written on it, so when he needed it, the appropriate verse would just fall down in front of his eyes." On hearing this, his sister, two years younger, quickly replied, "Stephan-Nelson, you are so bad that you might as well carry your whole Bible around with you."

Of course, we had a long way to go in teaching the art of encouragement, but we were thankful that at their young ages the children had seen and understood something of the importance of the Word of God in their everyday lives. Our children have learned that Scripture is a road map, an instruction book, and a reference point for our lives, and now they are passing these truths on to their own children.

The Word of God is vital to the quiet knowing we all long to experience. It is such a source of encouragement, especially during the long days in the valley or the desert times we all experience at one time or another. It is our source of encouragement, our reference point, the light for our path, our guidebook.

It has been said that God is the Eternal Contemporary. The Scriptures meet our needs at any given point in our lives. They have been meeting needs ever since God breathed His very own life into them.

*For you created my inmost being;
you knit me together in my mother's womb.
I praise you because I am
fearfully and wonderfully made.*

—Psalm 139:13–14

*Just as I am,
though tossed about
With many a conflict,
many a doubt,
Fightings and fears
within, without,
O Lamb of God
I come! I come!*

Just As I Am

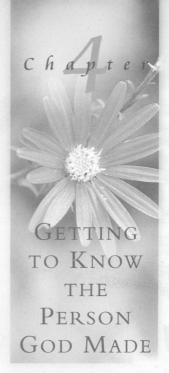

Chapter 4

GETTING TO KNOW THE PERSON GOD MADE

Have you ever wondered if God liked you? I have. Oh, I know that He loves me; the words to the precious hymn "Just As I Am" tell me that: "Just as I am thou wilt receive, . . . welcome, pardon, cleanse, relieve; because Thy promise I believe."

I know that He loves me, cleanses me, forgives me, and welcomes me just as I am, but I have not always been so sure that He likes me. Would God enjoy sitting on my porch watching the birds and squirrels squabble for the nuts and seeds I place there? Or would He like to go for a hike in the mountains with me just for the fun of it? I came to the conclusion that since I didn't particularly like myself, then He probably didn't particularly like me either.

I decided that I just wasn't His type. He says in Scripture that He likes a woman of "a gentle and quiet spirit" (1 Pet. 3:4), and I really don't quite fit that description. (As I mentioned earlier, it was years before I realized this verse had nothing to do with personality.)

At times we all struggle with a lack of self-confidence, maybe self-doubts. Maybe we just don't have a lot of self-esteem. This has been an ongoing struggle in my own life.

I have always thought that my mother was the most beautiful woman in the entire world. And not just beautiful, but perfect. I always knew that God really must like her; after all, everyone does. She is a woman of compassion; she is generous, unselfish, wise, and winsome with a great sense of humor and a wonderful witty, spunky personality. She radiates true beauty.

But the interesting thing is that she never has considered herself the least bit attractive. She sees herself as very plain and very ordinary. When she was dating Daddy, she wrote the following poem:

Your eyes
look down at me
so thoughtfully . . .
What do they see?
The plainness of me—
plainly built,
not small,
nor calmly poised,
nor quaint,
and, worst of all,
a nose upturned
and hands
that I have known
for years to be
too long,
too overgrown;
plain hazel eyes,
a face too pale,
not fair,
a mouth too large
and ordinary hair?
And all of me
tucked in
this homemade dress;
oh, if you look at me
so thoughtfully,
will you love me
the less?

—RUTH BELL GRAHAM

When I first read this poem, I was shocked. How could she think these things? Daddy has loved this little woman and has found her beauty far above anything he ever expected for almost sixty years.

I, too, have always struggled with having a sense of self-confidence and self-esteem. I just assumed, although I never doubted God's love for me, that He probably didn't find me particularly attractive nor would like to spend as much time with me as he did Mary or Bethany. I don't know why, that is just the way I felt. Maybe apples don't fall far from the tree and I get it from Mother. Who knows?

But, often with tears of longing I would sing the words to the hymn,

> And He walks with me, and He talks with me,
> And He tells me I am His own,
> And the joy we share as we tarry there,
> None other has ever known.[1]

How I envied the one who could write such beautiful words.

However, after years of struggling, I discovered that God not only loves me, but He rejoices over me with singing (see Zeph. 3:17), delights in me (see Ps. 147:11), desires me (see Song of Sol. 7:10), takes pleasure in me (see Ps. 149:4), accepts me (see Acts 10:35), and made me just the way I am—feisty personality, big mouth and all—for the purpose of glorifying Him and bringing Him pleasure.

Over the years, I have also found that my self-esteem and self-confidence grow in measure with my dependence on Him. And as long as I "snuggle instead of struggle," I can experience that quiet knowing of who I am and what I am in Him.

But He also allows circumstances, gives me experiences, and takes me down paths that are often difficult because He wants me to grow. Growing is not always easy, but it is the only way to blossom.

I find many people today who are looking for things that offer a certain measure of self-esteem and self-confidence in a variety of places—a job, spouse, higher education, etc. And while these things are good, they only offer limited satisfaction. Others seek self-esteem or fulfillment in the wrong places. They look for love, but they look for it in an affair. They seek security but seek it in a mate, job, or stock portfolio. They long for a sense of peace and serenity but seek it in a bottle of alcohol or pills. They desire self-esteem, so they acquire possessions and status symbols. One of the greatest examples Mother has been to me is of a woman who has not looked to anything or anyone to be to her what only Jesus Christ can be.

You see, all we need and desire, HE IS. At some point in each of our lives, God will bring us to a place where He will prove this to us.

I was just twelve years old the first time He brought me to this place in my life. I was sent away to boarding school in Central Florida. All my life until that point, I had lived in an idyllic community in the Blue Ridge Mountains of North Carolina. I was surrounded by wonderful men and women of God—happy, fun loving, balanced Christians—and I was dependent on them. I was dependent on our little church, that peaceful community, my family, and my grandparents who lived just across the street. But because the Lord wants to bring each one of us to a point in our lives where we're dependent on Him and Him alone, He led the path of my life to Florida.

I remember my family leaving me there on a hot and humid September day, the sand oozing into my sandals and the sweat rolling down my face, mingling with my tears. I watched their car drive away and felt totally abandoned. Soon a pain began to grow deep inside me called *homesickness*, which was very painful and extremely difficult. But I soon discovered something. I discovered that God did not live just in the mountains of North Carolina, but that He lived in Central Florida, too. I was there for four years, and it was during those years that Jesus became my very best friend.

At the age of seventeen, I married a man older than me, one whom I did not know well. We made our home in Switzerland, his home country. Suddenly, I was thrown into a world very different from anything I had ever known. I didn't speak the languages, I had no friends, we only had one car, my family was thousands of miles away, and communication with my family was extremely difficult. My father-in-law was a very controlling and abusive person, which caused many hardships and heartaches.

I soon learned French (a great motivation to learning a language is to have in-laws speaking in one that you do not understand). But one winter, when we were in a small Swiss-German village, my husband, Stephan, received a summons for several weeks of military service. When Stephan walked out the door, I threw myself down beside the bed in tears and cried out to the Lord that I didn't think I could take any more. As King David said, my spirit was overwhelmed and I felt so desolate (see Ps. 143:4).

I was in a village where I didn't understand a word, in a small apartment that had no heat. I had no car, no telephone, and no friends; my family was on the other side of the world; my in-laws were not speaking to me; my babies got sick; my husband was gone; and I was miserable.

Mother has always taught us by word and example never to expect anyone or anything to be to you that which only Jesus Christ can be.

Since I had nowhere to go and no one to turn to, I

turned to the Lord. Each day, as soon as I put the children down for their naps, I would sit in the kitchen near the wood stove, the only warm spot in the chalet, and pour out my heart to Him. I would then read all the verses of encouragement and comfort that I could find, especially in the Psalms and Isaiah and Jeremiah. In His presence, I began to prove the promises of God. By the time Stephan came back, several weeks later, I had learned the most important spiritual lesson I had ever learned. I found that when Jesus Christ is all you have, you soon discover that He is all you need.

And, each one of us has to come to a time and place in our lives where we learn to depend on Him and Him alone—not a particular church or pastor, not a Bible study, not a child, not a parent, not a friend, not even our mates. While these are all wonderful things, sometimes the Lord has to remove them from us or removes us from them in order to teach us to be dependent on Him and to prove to us that He is enough.

All we need and desire He is. He is the quiet knowing. Is He enough for you?

JUST AS I AM

Just as I am, without one plea,
But that Thy blood was shed for me,
And that Thou bidd'st me come to Thee,
O Lamb of God, I come! I come!

Just as I am, and waiting not
To rid my soul of one dark blot,
To Thee whose blood can cleanse each spot,
O Lamb of God, I come! I come!

Just as I am, tho' tossed about
With many a conflict, many a doubt,
Fightings within and fears without,
O Lamb of God, I come! I come!

Just as I am, poor, wretched, blind;
Sight, riches, healing of the mind,
Yea, all I need in Thee to find,
O Lamb of God, I come! I come!

Just as I am, Thou wilt receive,
Wilt welcome, pardon, cleanse, relieve;
Because Thy promise I believe,
O Lamb of God, I come! I come!

WORDS: CHARLOTTE ELLIOTT, 1789–1871

And the peace of God, which transcends all understanding, will guard your hearts and your minds in Christ Jesus.

—PHIL. 4:7

Thro' many dangers, toils, and snares,

I have already come;

'Tis grace has bro't me safe thus far,

And grace will lead me home.

Amazing Grace

GOD'S ALL-ENCOMPASSING PROVISION FOR US

John Newton's famous hymn "Amazing Grace" has been a source of encouragement for years because it is all about God's provision for us. For me personally, my whole life could be summed up by just two words, God's grace.

One aspect of God's amazing grace is that He accepts us just as we are. But to me, another amazing truth is that He loves us too much to leave us where He found us. God has brought many of His children through desert experiences, dense fog, and multiple storms, all because He loves us too much to leave us in the state in which He found us. And that is how we grow.

Our family home in the mountains of North Carolina has provided all of us with joy for almost half a century. Mother especially loves Little Piney Cove, where the comfortable, old rambling log home nestles in the arms of two hogback ridges. The smell of smoke from years of "laughing fires," the old brick floors, and polished primitive antique furniture, combined with local art and fresh flowers, all offer a warm welcome.

It seems like only yesterday that I was growing up there on that mountain, and now the grandchildren and great-grandchildren are roaming the trails, playing in the woods, looking for snakes, exploring the old cabin, and watching for the baby flying squirrel—drawn there by some unseen force of happy memories. It seems as if those old logs just sort of soak up the memories and laughter as well as the smell of wood smoke and cooking food.

Mother loves her Little Piney Cove, and this love is often reflected in her poems:

If I could have each day
one hour of sun,
glorious,
healing,
hot,
like now—
then
let Winter come!
Not
mild and brief,
but
wild, without relief;
let the storms rage,
let the winds blow,
the freezing rains
lashing my windowpanes;
then
let it snow!
long
and
deep
and cold.
I would not mind at all:
it would be fun . . .
if I could have
each day
my hour of sun.

—RUTH BELL GRAHAM

In many of these pieces of poetry, I detect a deeper meaning. Mother describes her physical earthly home in North Carolina, but she seems to go further and deeper, describing perhaps her spiritual home. In "If I Could Have Each Day," for example, she's not just talking about the sunshine we enjoy, but also that moment of intimacy with the Lord—that moment, that mountaintop experience. If we could just have that special moment, then let the storms of life come, the winds of uncertainty blow, the snows of sorrows and difficulties fall.

Job writes in the midst of all his troubles and sorrows, "When He gives quietness, who then can make trouble?" (Job 34:29 NKJV). If we possess that quiet knowing and have had that moment with the Son, then we, too, can face whatever comes in His strength and with a peace that passes understanding.

When I first went to Switzerland, I was a teenager. The beauty of the small country overwhelmed me—the spectacular views, the blue lakes dotted with tiny sailboats, the majestic snow-covered mountains, and the window boxes filled with flowers of every color. But one thing that really intrigued me was that we were near the timberline.

Being from North Carolina's Blue Ridge Mountains, I didn't know what a timberline was. Our beautiful mountains are covered with shrubs, trees, and growth of various kinds. How surprised I was to learn there are mountains so high that nothing much grows beyond a certain height!

The Swiss Alps, snowcapped even in summer, are spectacular. They thrill and elate all who are privileged to take in their beauty. Mother once described them in the following words:

Those
splendid, soaring
jagged peaks,
stripped of trees
of grass and sod
on whose snow
the sunlight lingers

are but the braille
letters, where we mortals
blind and fragile
trace our fingers
to spell the name
God.

—RUTH BELL GRAHAM

But as I began to explore their trails, I discovered that nothing much grows on those high, rugged peaks. A few lovely, rare flowers bloom on the mountaintops, but the majority of the planting, cultivating, pruning, growing, and fruit bearing takes place down in the valleys. These valleys are fertile and well tilled, yielding various and plentiful crops. Yet low-hanging clouds and fog often shroud these same valleys.

A few years later, when I married Stephan and made the Alps my home, this observation took on a new and more meaningful aspect. I began to see mountains and valleys in a spiritual context.

As a young bride adjusting to marriage and a strange country, away from all that was familiar, I began to experience days of disappointment, discouragement, loneliness, and despair. These experiences were not totally foreign to me. I had had such before. The difference was that this time I felt so alone. Stephan would leave in the morning to go to work, and a feeling of panic would begin to flood over me. The hours seemed like days. I would mercilessly clean to keep myself from thinking.

From time to time, I would gather all my courage and walk to the nearest little store, only to be met by a large, smiling woman who would rattle off, in French (which I did not understand), what seemed to be one hundred words a minute. I would be so intimidated that it would take a week for me to regain enough courage to try it again.

I wanted so much to fit in, to please. I not only wanted Stephan to be proud of me, but I wanted his family and friends to be proud of me as well. I tried so hard, and each time I goofed or made a faux pas (there were many), I cringed and longed to escape. I would often find myself in Stephan's arms, weeping frustrated tears. In spite of his efforts to encourage me and assure me that he was proud of me, I soon became deeply discouraged.

I felt confined to a life of living in valleys, and I grew weary of trying to climb out of the low-hanging fog of discouragement, loneliness, and despair that seemed so often to hide the mountain peaks. One of Mother's poems aptly describes how I felt during those days:

The hills on which I need to gaze
are wrapped in clouds again.
I lift up streaming eyes in vain
and feel upon my upturned face
the streaming rain.

—RUTH BELL GRAHAM

I even began to question if the mountains existed at all. I was trying so hard to climb out of the fog that I failed to recognize the opportunities for fruitfulness in the valleys. But all this time, my heavenly Gardener was using these valley times to prepare me, to cultivate me, to prune me, and to plant seeds that would one day yield fruit.

Isaiah 27:3 soon became one of my favorite verses. By changing the little word it to her or Gigi, it reads, "I, the LORD, watch over Gigi; I water her continually. I guard her day and night so that no one may harm her."

It wasn't long before I began to realize He was opening up springs in my valleys (scc Ps. 104:10). I would go through an especially difficult time and, looking back, would see I had experienced a very special time with the Gardener. I slowly began to realize and accept that He was using each of my valley experiences to achieve His plan and purpose for me, to bring me closer to Himself and bring honor to His name. I discovered He was cultivating me into a fruitful, watered garden and that He was becoming more and more the source of my satisfaction.

I have had many varied mountaintop experiences—

times when I have been able to rise above all that would normally cause me to be weary, times of spiritual refreshment, times of real encouragement, times of inner tranquillity, and times of peace and quiet. I thank the Lord for every one of them. But when I look back, I must admit it has been during the difficult days that I have learned to lean on the Lord. It is in these times I have learned to put my trust in Him and have found He is all I really need. It is in times like these that I search my Bible for answers, encouragement, and comfort.

I remember one chilly, foggy, drizzly day in our little Swiss village when the children wanted to go for a ride in the *tele cabine* that went straight up behind our chalet to the top of one of the mountain peaks. I agreed. We all bundled into a small cable car and soon were suspended high above the ground, moving slowly through the fog. Suddenly we broke through the clouds, and there, all around us, bathed in the warm sunshine, were glorious mountains. There are no words to describe this feeling. We stepped out onto a little terrace; sipped hot chocolate in the warm, soothing sun; and tried to capture forever in our memories the splendor of this experience.

All too soon, it was time to go, to return to the fog, the mundane, the frustrations, the difficulties, the daily valley life. We descended slowly, and sure enough, we were once again surrounded by low-hanging clouds as the mountains slipped from view. But I knew they were there. I had seen them. I had been encouraged. I turned to my valley with a renewed spirit and couldn't help realizing how similar this experience was to my spiritual life.

I might experience several dark, dreary days when I long to climb into the cable car and rise above it all, to break out of the fog and see life from a higher perspective. I hunger to experience that indescribable feeling of peace, security, power, stability, serenity—all that those mountains represent.

My mother, knowing how I felt, wrote these words for me while on a visit to Switzerland:

Above the clouds
thick, boiling, low,
appear the peaks
she came to know
as Father, Son,
and Holy Ghost.
Often when she
sought them most,
they would be hid
in clouds, from view.

Distraught by cares
she always knew,
silent, unseen
they still were there,
like God Himself—
unchanged, serene;
knowing this
she gathered strength
for each day's journey
—length by length.

—Ruth Bell Graham

Slowly but surely, I began to glimpse the obvious: We do have a way out of the fog, anytime we choose to rise above, to see the sun, to look at our valleys from a higher perspective. We can go directly to the source Himself to receive encouragement, strength, power, and "the peace of God, which transcends all understanding" (Phil. 4:7).

Both blessings and opportunities are discovered in clouds of fog. Scripture tells us "the glory of the LORD [appeared] in the cloud" (Exod. 16:10). Moses met God in the thick of a "dense cloud" (Exod. 19:9). We also discover His promises in the clouds. He says in Genesis 9:13 that He set His bow (the rainbow of promise) in the cloud.

So we should thank the Lord for the foggy times, the clouds, the difficult times, the storms of life. But we should also be thankful for the sunshine. If every now and then He gives us one moment of sun, one glimpse of the glorious mountaintops, then we can go back down into the fog-shrouded valley strengthened and encouraged to face the inevitable storms that await us. That glimpse of sun will be enough to give us the quiet knowing of His presence that, although at times is hidden, is never far away.

What joy and peace we experience when we have that quiet knowing and assurance that He will never lead us where His amazing grace will not keep us.

AMAZING GRACE

Amazing grace! How sweet the sound,
That saved a wretch like me!
I once was lost, but now am found,
Was blind, but now I see.

'Twas grace that taught my heart to fear,
And grace my fears relieved;
How precious did that grace appear
The hour I first believed!

Thro' many dangers, toils, and snares,
I have already come;
'Tis grace hath bro't me safe thus far,
And grace will lead me home.

The Lord has promised good to me,
His word my hope secures;
He will my shield and portion be
As long as life endures.

When we've been there ten thousand years,
Bright shining as the sun,
We've no less days to sing God's praise
Than when we first begun.

WORDS: ST. 1–4, JOHN NEWTON, 1725–1807;
ST. 5, ANONYMOUS C. 1790.

This is love: not that we loved God, but that he loved us and sent his Son as an atoning sacrifice for our sins.

—1 John 4:10

Love divine, all loves excelling

Joy of heav'n, to earth come down;

Fix in us Thy humble dwelling;

All Thy faithful mercies crown.

Love Divine

A GLIMPSE OF DIVINE LOVE

There is no greater love than the love of God. However, here on earth God has given us certain relationships that give us a taste of or a glimpse into His divine love.

The first relationship that was created and ordained by God to help us understand in some small measure the greatness of His love is the marriage relationship. A well-balanced, loving marriage relationship is the nearest thing to "heaven on earth," as so many of our writers have reminded us. Scripture includes many comparisons between our relationship with God and the marriage relationship.

I believe that one of the reasons that I came to know and love the Lord at an early age was because I saw His love manifest in the marriage relationships around me. From the time I was a very young girl, I knew Mother and Daddy loved each other. They were obviously sweethearts, and after almost sixty years of marriage, they are lovers still.

Mother penned this about her hero:

I met you years ago
when
of all the men
I knew,
you,
I hero-worshiped
then:
you are my husband now.
my husband!

and from my home
(your arms),
I turn to look
down the long trail of years
to where I met you first
and hero-worshiped,
and I would smile;
. . . I know you better now:
the faults,

the odd preferments,
the differences
that make you you.
That other me
—so young,
so far away—
saw you
and hero-worshiped

but never knew;
while I,
grown wiser
with the closeness of these years,
hero-worship, too!

—RUTH BELL GRAHAM

Mother and Daddy's marriage is an exception and not necessarily an example. God picked a very special woman and a very special man to do a very special job. Young Christians today can't look at Ruth and Billy Graham as an example of a "normal" marriage. So in that sense, I don't know whether I was fortunate or unfortunate. But from the moment I could sense things, I knew Mother and Daddy loved each other deeply and dearly. Even today in their older age, whenever I'm with them, Daddy's eyes light up and his whole demeanor changes when Mother is in the room. And Mother's eyes light up and she becomes happy and excited when he comes into the room. So I know there is a real love match there. It was a great sacrifice for them to be apart so much of the time because they were and are deeply in love.

In looking at Mother as a wife, as well as the other women we grew up around, there was balance. As a young girl I was taught by my mother never to marry a man I was not willing to adjust to. Paul tells us in Ephesians that in marriage, we are to submit (adjust) to one another. Marriage is the joining together of two very different people as iron sharpens iron. So there has to be a willingness to adjust to one another, a mutual submitting in love. And there is commitment. I believe that this is the most important thing I have learned by observing my grandparents' and my parents' marriages.

Life was not always easy. My paternal grandparents had a dairy farm. This meant long days and lots of hard work. My grandmother, "Mother Graham," birthed five children. She got up each morning long before dawn and fixed an old-fashioned Southern breakfast not only for her family, but for the farmhands as well. There was not only the hard work and long days, but the Depression, financial concerns, and the loss of a child, as well as everyday pressures and burdens. But, above all, there was commitment.

My mother's parents married young and then went immediately to China as medical missionaries. Life was hard. They were far from all that was familiar and dear. It took weeks to receive a letter from family and friends. They, too, lost a little boy. There were not only the pressures and responsibilities of the hospital, but the

compound and the family. There were bandits, wars, sick-
nesses, and loneliness, but there was also commitment.

Years later, when my grandmother Bell was confined
to a wheelchair, my mother entered their room and found
my grandfather on his knees, putting my grandmother's
stockings on her. He looked up at Mother and said, "This
is the greatest privilege of my life." This is just one example
of his commitment to his beloved wife.

One of the major magazines came out with an issue of
the one hundred greatest love stories of the century. All
kinds of celebrities were featured. And tucked in with the
rest was a very small picture of Mother and Daddy. I
looked at the other "great love stories" and thought,
Most of these so-called love stories have ended in divorce, and

many are not even married, so what exactly does this culture perceive as love?

Here is a couple who have been married almost sixty years, still together and still in love. They have endured ups and downs, hardships, stress, separations, sadness, and loneliness, as well as happy times. And their love story is tucked in between notorious love stories that have not lasted. Which is the true example of love?

As I've said before, Mother always reminds us not to expect anyone or anything to be to you what only Jesus Christ can be. So she never expected Daddy to fulfill her every need. She never expected him or their marriage to be perfect. I think many women, perhaps because of Hollywood's perspective on love and marriage, expect too much out of marriage. Yet, when you go back to Genesis, when God created a man and a woman and put them together, it seems to me He did it mainly for two reasons. One was for procreation and the other was for companionship. And we've made marriage into so much more that we're bound to set ourselves up for disappointment.

The late Robert Quinlan once described marriage as "the union of two good forgivers." As I understand it, there are two areas in which forgiveness is needed in marriage. First, there are the daily irritations and annoyances that we experience in marriage. Some of these simply need to be overlooked. Others need to be addressed and discussed so that these small irritations and offenses won't build into resentfulness and bitterness. We need to offer daily forgiveness of those minor irritations, with which most of us can readily identify.

For instance, not long ago, I was preparing to leave to speak at a nearby conference. I asked Stephan if he would load several boxes of books into the trunk of my car, as I have a bad back, and lifting heavy boxes might mean spending the next week in bed. "I'll do it in a few minutes, honey," he replied, intently watching the evening news.

Stephan tends to be forgetful, so it wasn't surprising that, after the news was over, he forgot my request. So I asked him again. Yet, by bedtime, the books were still not in the car.

"Honey," I said, "let's go out and put those boxes in the car. It settles my mind to know they're in the car."

"I told you," Stephan said a bit impatiently, "I'll do it. Those boxes will be in your car before you leave tomorrow morning."

I decided not to say another word. Yet, the next morning, the boxes were still in the hallway and Stephan had already gone to his office. I lifted them into the trunk, bad back and all, and went off to my conference— frustrated and hurt.

A few days later, Stephan came to me and apologized. "Gigi," he said, "I was sitting in the middle of a counseling session when it suddenly dawned on me that I'd forgotten to put those books in your car. I'm really sorry."

Forgetfulness, misunderstandings, and a thousand other irritants have a way of cutting at a marriage. But how we treat those annoyances can mean the difference between temporary unpleasantness and long-term hurt.

I accepted Stephan's apology. After thirty-eight years of marriage, I knew he didn't mean to hurt me, and I knew that not accepting his apology could have resulted in additional anger, hurt feelings, and bitterness—not exactly the ingredients of a happy marriage. After all, Proverbs 10:12 tells us, "Hatred stirs up dissension, but love covers over all wrongs." In other words, love chooses to forget.

Many of the mosquitoes in a marriage can be swatted away by fostering a "get-over-it" attitude. Take the box episode I just described. Sure, I was angry and frustrated. Stephan should have done what I asked. And I could have let my irritation over the incident brew, but I made myself stop and listen to common sense: Are forgotten boxes really worth a major marital dissension?

I'm convinced that one of Satan's tricks is to close our minds to common sense. When that happens, we soon find ourselves consumed by minor offenses. And I know how easily that can happen. The entire way to the airport that day, all I could think about was, *Why couldn't Stephan have helped me with my simple request? Why does he have to be so forgetful? If he really loves me, he would have loaded those boxes.*

Instead of thinking about the women to whom I would be ministering, I was indulging in a "pity party." I was brooding over something of only momentary importance, which over time would be of little importance. I needed to simply accept Stephan's apology and say, "These things happen. That's life." Then I needed to let go.

Someone once said that being a good parent is learning when to choose to ignore things. The same can be said about a good marriage partner. As hard as it might seem now, we have to make a conscious decision to let go. We can move beyond those daily, minor irritations by simply choosing to ignore or at least choosing not to concentrate on the small infractions, and then zero in on the positive aspects. I once heard a pastor say, "Eliminate the negatives by accentuating the positives." How true this is in a loving marriage.

Of course, this doesn't mean little irritations should not be addressed. Every marriage experiences times when a husband or a wife goes through weeks—maybe months—when everything about the other person bothers him or her. But when these little irritations begin to multiply, we need to be on the lookout for signs of bitterness building up in our relationships. When this happens, just "getting over it" is not enough. We may need to discuss it with our spouses to better understand each other.

For instance, if Stephan's forgetfulness became an ongoing nuisance, I owe it to our relationship to bring it to his attention. Perhaps I need to take him out to dinner and say, "Honey, I need to talk to you. In the past four weeks, I have nicely asked you to do several things. Yet, you always seem to forget and I'm a little hurt. I feel as though you're always putting others first."

This will give us the opportunity to discuss openly what bothers us and try to find the cause of the irritant. It will also help us begin to correct it. Openly discussing small irritants is so much better than stuffing them further inside until frustration builds into a blowup.

The second occasion when forgiveness is needed is when a serious wrong, like physical abuse or adultery, has occurred in a marriage. Sadly, I think many of us have been taught a lopsided view of forgiveness. We constantly hear about the importance of unconditional forgiveness, yet what is overlooked is repentance. God does not forgive us until we ask Him to forgive. He stands ready to forgive—His arms are open wide. But that circle of forgiveness cannot be complete until we ask Him to forgive us. If a woman's husband has been unfaithful, she can be ready and willing to forgive him, but if he has never asked for forgiveness, the circle is not complete.

Also, in some circumstances, there can be real and complete forgiveness without reconciliation. Again, we are living in an imperfect world with imperfect people affected by the fall. Consequently, some marriages have been broken and cannot be repaired although forgiveness has taken place.

No matter if we're talking about forgiveness of myriad "nuisances" or a major wrong in our marriages, we need to understand that forgiveness can't be based on feelings. Our feelings change. Forgiveness, however, is an act of obedience. If we have forgiven, we can't rely on feelings. Satan will come along and say, "You didn't really forgive that person. Remember all

those terrible feelings you had when you thought about that person today?"

One way I measure my forgiveness is by gauging my bitterness level. If I feed a sense of bitterness, then I know I've not truly forgiven. While often we still feed pain or sadness after we've offered forgiveness, bitterness has to go. Bitterness is something that gnaws at you, something that can grow and eventually consume you and destroy any relationship, especially a marriage.

I have a friend who went through a divorce a number of years ago. I received a letter from her recently and could sense she was consumed by bitterness—over her divorce, over the settlement, and over the fact that her ex-husband is remarried and has a child. She's engulfed by bitterness. She may see her ex-husband in the mall one day and experience all kinds of emotions. That's OK;

that's normal. But forgiveness is living free of consuming bitterness.

Not allowing bitterness to take hold requires hard work. I know a couple who has made their marriage work, despite the husband's extramarital affair. The wife chose to stay in the marriage because she remembered how wonderful it was before. It was something she wanted back. But I know for her the cost of forgiveness is a day-to-day thing. It means making a real effort not to remember, not to grieve over what happened, not to bring it up . . . but to move on, just as the Lord does with us. When we have asked His forgiveness, He is merciful and remembers it no more (see Jer. 31:34; Heb. 8:12).

One misconception surrounding forgiveness is that once given, everything ends "happily ever after." Not so. Forgiveness does not eradicate the consequences of our sins. Rather, it provides two people the means to deal with those consequences.

In another marriage I know of, the husband is very repentant for his nearly five years of infidelity. And the wife has forgiven her husband for this serious breach in their marriage. But the foundations of the relationship were so damaged it simply couldn't be repaired, and eventually they divorced. There was no storybook ending here, but because of forgiveness, the couple is not absorbed in bitterness over the situation. Yet, they still had to live with the sad consequences of sin—a broken marriage.

Remember, a good marriage is made up of two good forgivers. One of my favorite verses on marriage is Ephesians 4:32: "Be kind and compassionate to one another, forgiving each other, just as in Christ God forgave you." Forgiveness starts with a humble heart. This doesn't mean simply accepting every wrong done to us or avoiding any loving confrontation of a wrong done too many times. Rather, it means understanding that we, like our spouses, have been forgiven much. And with that perspective, it puts us both on an equal footing.

Added to the humble hearts we bring to our marriages should be our own commitments to the marriage. I'm married to Stephan for a lifetime. With this perspective, it's to our benefit to do what we can to keep our relationship running smoothly and growing in love, not bitterness and resentment. Forgiveness makes that possible.

Marriage is not easy. It is a relationship. And all relationships are complex and sometimes even complicated. Marriage is not so much "warm fuzzy feelings" as it is faithfulness to the process of growing together. A good marriage does not necessarily mean an absence of conflict, but a determination to resolve the conflicts. It is commitment—commitment first of all to the Lord, then a commitment to the institution of marriage, and finally a commitment to each other. Marriage, after all, was the first institution created and ordained by God.

When I got married at seventeen, I had no idea what I was getting into. But the morning of my wedding day, my daddy gave me a note. It began, "And there was a marriage in Cana of Galilee, and Jesus was there."

At the marriage in Cana, Jesus was not only there, but He performed a miracle. If Jesus is in our marriages, we can experience a quiet knowing, because miracles, some small and some large, will take place. In fact, problems can be the platform from which God will perform a miracle. But we must also have commitment.

Remember, lasting marriages don't just happen. They are made up of both commitment and miracles.

LOVE DIVINE, ALL LOVES EXCELLING

Love divine, all loves excelling,
Joy of heav'n, to earth come down;
Fix in us Thy humble dwelling;
All Thy faithful mercies crown!
Jesus, Thou art all compassion,
Pure, unbounded love Thou art;
Visit us with Thy salvation;
Enter ev'ry trembling heart.

Breathe, O breathe Thy loving Spirit,
Into ev'ry troubled breast!
Let us all in Thee inherit,
Let us find the promised rest;
Take away our bent to sinning;
Alpha and Omega be;
End of faith, as its beginning,
Set our hearts at liberty.

Come, Almighty to deliver,
Let us all Thy grace receive;
Suddenly return, and never,
Nevermore Thy temples leave.
Thee we would be always blessing,
Serve Thee as Thy hosts above,
Pray and praise Thee without ceasing,
Glory in Thy perfect love.

WORDS: CHARLES WESLEY, 1707–1788

He who dwells in the shelter of the Most High will rest in the shadow of the Almighty.

—Psalm 91:1

Jesus loves me! this I know,

For the Bible tells me so;

Little ones to Him belong;

They are weak, but He is strong.

Chapter 7

Little Ones to Him Belong

BUSYNESS AND MOTHERING

My first impression of Jesus was my mother. I could have sung this song, "Jesus loves me, this I know, for my mother shows me so."

Mother never considered it a sacrifice to stay home with us children. We were all full of life and quite a handful; however, though she never complained, I think at times that it must have been difficult. Knowing that her husband was traveling the world, meeting interesting people, seeing exciting places, and doing what many considered a great work for the Lord, she must have every now and then felt "confined" to the mountains of North

Carolina, with five small children and all that this entailed. I never realized just how hard this must have been until I had my seven.

Mother has often been asked how she raised us with Daddy being gone so much of the time. Her immediate reply has always been, "On my knees." The Gospel of Matthew reminds us that when we've done it unto the least of these, we've done it for Him (see Matt. 25:40). And I believe the ministry of staying home and caring for children is one of the greatest ministries God entrusts to His children.

Mother was a great example of a balanced mother. I think of the things she passed on to me, and I in turn, to my children. The example of her dependence on, and her relationship with, a personal God gave me the strength I needed to raise seven children. As she has said, she raised her children on her knees. Prayer was a vital part of her life. Knowing that prayer was her stronghold, her shelter, and her anchor was also a great example to me.

She never sacrificed her family on the altar of public opinion. I firmly believe, especially in Christian families, that there is more concern about maintaining an image than about working on a problem, which tends to cause a lot of dysfunction. We don't want to admit having problems, or maybe we think that Christians shouldn't have certain problems. We don't want to admit that we have failed, that we don't have it all together, or that we are suffering from doubts or depression.

I don't think children are looking for perfection in their parents; they're looking for reality. We have to be as real and honest and transparent as we can be in front of our families and friends, letting them know that we make mistakes and sometimes fail and that they're going to make mistakes and sometimes fail, too. But we must remind them that we're there to love and encourage one another and that, for a Christian, failure is not final.

I think that Mother provided us also with a sense of security. She didn't always approve of what we did, but we knew she approved of us, and that was a wonderful lesson for me as a mother. When I had a prodigal son, I was able to separate what he did from who he was. I was able to love him but hate the lifestyle he was living.

As a parent, Mother tried not to major on non-essential issues or nonmoral issues. She was strong on moral issues, such as respect, truthfulness, honesty, and sexual morality, but she didn't focus on hairstyles, piercings, skirt lengths, makeup, or even clean rooms. These were not major issues. I think we as parents sometimes make the mistake of spending too much time on nonessential things.

Because of the difficulties my siblings and I gave our mother, with Daddy gone, I am amazed how "together" spiritually Mother seemed to those around her. We weren't angels (most people know this because of what she's written about us), and Daddy's absences must have created many difficult times for her. She was a very busy

woman with many pressures and responsibilities, but to the world and us, she seemed "together." She describes those busy days of motherhood in one of her poems:

God,
bless all young mothers
at end of day,
kneeling wearily with each
small one
to hear them pray.
Too tired to rise when done . . .
and yet, they do,
longing just to sleep
one whole night through.

Too tired to sleep . . .
too tired to pray . . .
God,
bless all young mothers
at close of day.

—RUTH BELL GRAHAM

Many mothers today find our daily lives so hectic. Where does it stop? There seems to be no end to the demands and expectations placed on parents today. We are all plagued by time pressure. I am sure all of us have felt, at one time or another, that everything is coming in on us, that we are never finished, never caught up. As the queen in Alice in Wonderland said, "It takes all the running you can do to stay in place. If you want to get someplace else, you must run twice as fast as that." How true this is for me. I have a difficult time admitting that I don't have it all together or that I can't do it all. But, I am learning. I sometimes find myself running in circles or running in place; and if I take a moment to ask why, I can't find a good reason.

Being too busy has become a compulsion for many and a way of life for most. The effects of busyness are becoming more and more evident. How many of us suffer from tension in one form or another? How many of us are difficult to live with because we are just plain overworked and overtired? We haven't learned, nor are we willing to learn to accept our limits.

I have a hard time believing this kind of busyness is pleasing to the Lord, and yet, it is a battle I have to fight constantly. To my discouragement, I frequently find myself on the losing side. How often I have been so busy that I have failed to encourage someone or forgotten to thank and praise a child for a job well done or failed to take the time to be with someone who just needed a friend. How often I have been running around so much all day that I am too preoccupied to be attentive to my children when they arrive home or too tired to be loving to my husband when he comes home depleted. I wrote the following poem to describe this constant battle I have with busyness:

Nerves

Tears

Tension

Pressures

Running all about

It all builds up

We can only take so much

And then begin to doubt.

We start to fall apart

With a start,

We begin to realize

How we feel

How we react.

We become afraid

We don't know ourselves

We find we lack

The strength and courage

We used to have.

We long for a new lease on life

But it doesn't

Instead,

Inside strife continues

We begin to reexamine.

We are all confused

We feel so unused.

So,

Tired

Weary,

Eyes bleary

I ask

Why?

—GIGI TCHIVIDJIAN

Yes, daily life is a battle, and I have come to believe it is a spiritual battle. Someone once said if the devil can't make you bad, he makes you busy. How true this is. But how do we handle our busy schedules? How do we respond to all the needs? How do we answer all the requests? Are we to say yes each time we are asked to serve in some capacity? Are we to walk through every open door? The needs are so great, and there is no end to all we could be involved with—good, important, positive, helpful, spiritual activities. But where do we draw the line? Are we just to grin and bear it and go on until we collapse in a heap on the floor?

I know many people who equate busyness and activity with spirituality. The busier someone is, the more spiritual she appears. Often, her morale is boosted and ego fed when others ask, "How do you do it? How do you find the time and energy?"

But is this really pleasing to the Lord? Is this what He really expects from us?

The Lord tells us, through the pen of Solomon in Proverbs 31:16, that the ideal woman "considers a new field before she buys or accepts it—expanding prudently [and not courting neglect of her present duties by assuming others]. With her savings [of time and strength] she plants fruitful vines in her vineyard" (AMP).

Mother has been a very fruitful woman. She has led a full and busy life. Although she had help, she also bore many responsibilities on her shoulders alone. However when I think of Mother, I don't have the image of a harried, worn-out, nervous, overextended woman. She somehow managed, with God's help, to maintain a sense of calm in the midst of her busy, demanding life. I believe it had a lot to do with a quiet knowing; she knew the certainties that she had as her priorities.

I constantly struggle with my priorities. I think they are all in order, and then I find that in a very short time, I have to work on them again. Plus I am sure that I have attention deficit disorder. These disorders were not discovered when I was young, but I start five major projects all at one time, and my mind goes in ten directions at once, jumping from one thing to another so quickly that I can't even keep up. Consequently, I tend to become too busy very quickly.

Being too busy is enemy number one to my to-do list.

I get talked into so many good things. One of the most difficult things for me is to say no to something or someone. Yet when I look at my list, whether mental or written, and examine it before the Lord, I often have to say no in order to be obedient to Him. He has given each of us the ability and freedom to say no; we just don't use it.

Thomas á Kempis reminds us that, just as it is often our duty to do what we don't particularly want to do, it is also our duty at times to leave undone what we want to do. Making and keeping our priorities in order and balanced takes a conscious effort and involves making conscious decisions.

Many of the demands on our lives are necessary and have to be dealt with accordingly. If you have a family, you have to care for them, feed them, bathe them, etc. If you have a job, you have to show up on time, pick up your children from school at a set hour, buy groceries, and wash clothes. Bills have to be paid and lawns mowed. And all of these things take time.

Sometimes I long for the sun to stand still. Yet I know that if He did stop the sun for me, I would just add more and more to my schedule, and my problems would increase instead of decrease. In reality, there is just so much time in each day and so much energy in each of us. God does not give us more to do than we can get done. If we are overburdened by busyness, then we need to reexamine our schedules and commitments.

We also must allow for our personal levels of energy, emotional as well as physical. We must allow for personal abilities and limitations. It is just as important to know what our gifts and abilities are not as well as what they are. In Ephesians 2:10 we read, "For we are God's workmanship, created in Christ Jesus to do good works, which God prepared in advance for us to do." This means God has a plan for each of us. God has prepared an agenda for our lives. To me, this is so encouraging and thrilling: Not only does God have a plan for me and for my life, but He cares so much for me that He prepared this plan in advance.

Although He has a unique plan for each of our lives, He has given each of us the same capability of faithfulness. That is His only requirement—not perfection, but faithfulness. The rush of "other things" tends to obscure His will and His values. This is why I have found it so important to examine my priorities very honestly before Him. It is not always easy to know what commitments should be on my to-do list or in which order to place them.

We live in constant tension with what we perceive as urgent and what is really important. My daddy's favorite chorus when I was a small girl was:

> With eternity's values in view, Lord,
> with eternity's values in view.
> Let me do each day's work for Jesus
> with eternity's values in view.

I often wonder, What is of real importance from eternity's perspective? This helps me put in balance the many pressures that encroach on my day.

I think that when we get to heaven, we are going to have a few surprises. Perhaps I will find that the phone call that interrupted my writing and put me behind was more important than my deadline. Maybe the woman who wanted to pour out her heart in the grocery store was more important than having dinner on time. Maybe putting the broom down and reading to my grandchild was more important than cleaning the house.

A very interesting study is to take the Gospels and find each time that Jesus was interrupted. How many miracles took place because of an interruption?

I remember on one occasion reexamining my list while I was sitting in a doctor's office. I was reading a book on the Psalms, and I came across Psalm 1:3: "He is like a tree planted by streams of water, which yields its fruit in season and whose leaf does not wither. Whatever he does prospers."

There it was, right in front of me. With seven children,

it was obvious that my season, for that time, was home-making and mothering. It was there that I would bring forth my fruit. It was there that I would prosper. This verse also says the tree was planted by streams of water, so I knew that, on top of the list, I had to put "residing near the Source." If I was to receive strength to bring forth good fruit and be productive in the home and prosper in my efforts, I had to abide in the One who said, "If anyone is thirsty, let him come to me and drink" (John 7:37).

But circumstances change, children grow up, and responsibilities shift. With most of our children now married with children of their own, I have found I have a little more time for other interests. There are things I have always wanted to do and now I have a little time to pursue some of them. I have always wanted to learn to shoot, ride a motorcycle, skydive, and dance. I also enjoy the opportunities I have to write, speak, and work on various projects that stretch me. I also love the work I do with the Ruth and Billy Graham Children's Health Center. I have fifteen grandchildren and am often called on to baby-sit, which I thoroughly enjoy. I still have a teenage son who needs direction and encouragement, elderly parents whom I long to spend time with, and friends I haven't seen for months, as well as a loving husband who wants a wife. Yes, there is so much to do and so little time with which to do it.

But I believe that if we abide daily in Him and in His Word and seek with all our hearts to do His will, then by faith we can rest assured that we are following His plan for our lives. How sad it would be to get so busy and so involved in our own activities that we completely miss His plan for us!

We somehow assume as Christians that service is what we do, but really, service is what we are. To be is so much more important than to do. To all who are too tired to sleep and too tired to pray, remember the following:

> It is not in doing but in being
> It is not in trying but in trusting
> It is not in rushing but in resting
> That we find the strength of the Lord.
> —UNKNOWN

JESUS LOVES ME

Jesus loves me! this I know,
For the Bible tells me so;
Little ones to him belong;
They are weak, but He is strong.

REFRAIN:
Yes, Jesus loves me,
Yes, Jesus loves me,
Yes, Jesus loves me,
The Bible tells me so.

Jesus loves me! He who died
Heaven's gates to open wide!
He will wash away my sin,
Let His little child come in.
(refrain)

Jesus loves me! loves me still,
Tho' I'm very weak and ill;
From His shining throne on high,
Comes to watch me where I lie.
(refrain)

Jesus loves me! He will stay
Close beside me all the way;
If I love Him, when I die
He will take me home on high.
(refrain)

WORDS: ANNA B. WARNER, 1820–1915

Though you have made me see troubles, many and bitter, you will restore my life again; from the depths of the earth you will again bring me up. You will increase my honor and comfort me once again.

—Psalm 71:20–21

"Lord, Thou hast here Thy ninety and nine;

Are they not enough for Thee?"

But the Shepherd made answer:

"This of mine

Has wandered away from me,

And altho' the road be rough and steep,

I go to the desert to find my sheep,

I go to the desert to find my sheep."

Chapter 8

The Ninety and Nine

WORRYING ABOUT A LOST CHILD

I watched my son as he walked down the driveway and out into the road. I continued watching until he rounded the corner until I could no longer see him. Tears stung as I realized that I might never see him again, that he might not ever come back.

What had gone wrong? We all know a prodigal. Prodigals come in all sizes and shapes. There are prodigal sons, prodigal daughters, fathers, mothers, husbands, prodigal sisters, brothers, prodigal friends.

One warm, balmy evening, Mother and I were in Florida, where she was to be interviewed at an event honoring a prestigious medical institution. The waves gently lapped the white sand beach outside of our hotel room, and the palm fronds rustled against the window as we dressed for dinner.

During the interview that evening, she answered questions about her childhood in China, her high-school years in North Korea, and then her marriage to, and her life with, my daddy, Billy Graham. She went on to discuss her years as a mother, her joys as well as her difficulties. She talked about the times of having to make decisions when Daddy was away preaching, sometimes tough decisions, alone. She also shared about the trying, difficult years when she had to deal with her prodigal.

After dinner, many came up to thank Mother for her honest, open sharing. I noticed a distinguished, well-dressed woman who hung back, waiting for a chance to speak. Tension was evident and she struggled to hold back the tears. When the crowd cleared, she approached Mother timidly, hesitantly.

"My son died of an overdose of drugs," she said with difficulty. "Do you think I will see him again in heaven?"

Of course, Mother didn't know any of the details, but she saw before her a mother with a very heavy heart. So she answered, "If you heard a timid knock on your door one day, and you answered the knock only to find your child standing there, bruised, wounded, bleeding, dirty, and tattered, what would you do? Slam the door in his face? Or would you throw open the door and welcome him into your arms?"

Suddenly, this mother's face registered relief. I saw the load lift from her shoulders as the tears flowed down her cheeks because she knew she was hearing from a mother who knew what it was like to have a prodigal. They hugged each other, and the woman turned and disappeared into the crowd.

Mother has always been a true example of what I firmly believe that the New Testament teaches: Our job is to love; it's the Holy Spirit's job to convict and God's job to judge.

Mother and I both have shared some of the struggles we experienced while waiting for our prodigals to return. Her book *Prodigals and Those Who Love Them* documents some of these. Of all the subjects in her hundreds of poems, it is the theme of the prodigal she returns to again and again:

Like other shepherds
help me keep
watch over my flock by night;
mindful of each need,
each hurt, which might
lead one to stray,
each weakness
and each ill—
while others sleep
teach me to pray.
At night the wolves
    and leopards,
hungry and clever, prowl
in search of strays.
and wounded; when
        they howl,
Lord, still
my anxious heart
to calm delight—
for the Great Shepherd
watches with me
over my flock
by night.

—RUTH BELL GRAHAM

One of the endearing things about Mother's writing is the way she shows how she tends to vacillate between her own human worry and concern and the knowledge that a sovereign God is in charge. It seems a contradiction to say you can have a quiet knowing when a child has left home or is lost and you have no control, whatsoever. I know, because I've had a prodigal and have been helped by the duality of the example Mother set, that of a mother's natural worry and at the same time her dependence on God.

My heart still aches within me, though, when I remember standing in the doorway, watching my son walk slowly down the street. After a few minutes, with a heart that felt heavy as lead, I reluctantly turned away.

I remember forcing myself to go through the motions of fixing dinner and doing the evening chores. When I finally crawled into bed, I lay awake, crying and wondering about my son. Where was he? Had he eaten supper? Did he have a place to sleep? Could we have done things differently? Would he ever come home again?

I thought back over the months. The ups and downs,

the emotions, the harsh words, the frustrations, the disobedience, the dishonesty, the questions, the long nights . . . sitting and waiting, wondering, worrying, asking, "Why?"

Unable to control the tears, I thought about all the chances we had given our son. We had taken him back repeatedly, only to have him abuse our trust and disrupt our family life. We had done all we knew to do until finally, tonight, because of the other children, my husband had to ask him to leave our home.

I wasn't prepared for a prodigal. I never imagined I would one night lie in bed, wondering where my son was. But once you love, you are never free again, and the Lord used this heartbreaking situation to teach me many things. I had to cope with overwhelming sadness that at times almost engulfed me.

After years of our giving all we had to this beloved child, he chose to disregard his training and reject his teaching. But as painful as it was, Stephan and I also realized we could not allow the behavior of this one child to consume us. At times we had to purposefully put our prodigal out of our minds. It simply wasn't fair to focus all our attention and emotional energy on him at the expense of the other members of the family.

I have also had to deal with guilt. During the first few months and many times afterward, I experienced searing stabs of guilt and self-doubt. Could I have brought him up differently? Had I been too strict—or not strict enough? Had I shown him enough love? Had I truly gone the extra mile?

I know I made mistakes, but I also know I did my best. So I had to recognize these stabs of guilt for what they were—attacks of Satan to discourage and paralyze me. At times the Lord had to gently remind me to deal with my son as He deals with His children: to keep the doors of communication always open, to accept the person, even when I could not accept his actions and conduct.

Sometimes accomplishing this was terribly difficult. I had to ask the Lord for His wisdom and discernment in knowing how to demonstrate love to my son without approving of his behavior. The Lord reminded me that sometimes love has to be tough. Sometimes lessons are only learned the hard way. I also had to be careful not to interfere with God's dealings in my son's life, allowing him to suffer the consequences of his choices and actions—even though my mother's heart wanted to shield him.

I also had to deal with repeated disappointment. My emotions felt as if they'd been jerked along on a carnival ride. Up. Down. High. Low. Soaring. Crashing. From time to time the situation seemed improved, the tensions less, my son's attitude different. I was encouraged, and my hopes rose—hopes that he would keep his job, go back to school, be sorry, change his ways, and even come home again. But soon we would experience yet another disappointment.

The telephone would ring and it would be Daddy. "How is Tullian?" he would ask. I would express to him my frustration and disappointment, and he would sweetly say, "Honey, love and patience, love and patience."

The Lord is the Author of hope. The greatest lesson I had to learn was to release my white-knuckled grip and to allow God to be in control of these circumstances. The Lord wants us to be totally dependent on Him every minute of every day, and He chose this situation in my life to teach me once again that He is able.

Stephan says that patience is faith seeing the finished product. Andrew Wyeth, the American artist, once said that the most irritating experience for an artist is to have his work criticized before it is finished. If you have a

prodigal—a son, daughter, husband, father, mother, or wife who is wandering spiritually—be persistent in prayer, and be patient. And be encouraged! Remember, God is not finished.

I would like to share two poems written March 7, 1989, the night Tullian left home:

I sit and wait . . . wondering . . .
My child is late.
And my mother's heart is worried.
All is quiet . . . all is still.
All but my anxious heart.
And as my eyes fill up and spill the tears
Upon my upturned face,
I ask, "Lord, give me grace."

* * *

Lord, bring him back.
Please bring him back
into this land again.
But while he is away
With him closely stay.
And bring peace to my troubled heart.
Let the tears that start

Each day to flow
Be turned into a prayer
Because I do not know
What to do . . . Where to start!
Lord, please take
A worried mother's heart
As an offering today
And bring my boy home to stay.

By God's grace, Tullian's story has a happy ending. And if you're a mother, worrying about your child, I pray, also, for a happy ending for you. However, I have friends whose prodigals have not returned and some who have lost their prodigals to accidents; yet their faith and trust in a sovereign God remains strong. If you find yourself in this situation, remember this precious promise from our Lord: "Blessed are those who have not seen and yet have believed" (John 20:29 NIV).

THE NINETY AND NINE

There were ninety and nine that safely lay
In the shelter of the fold,
But one was out on the hills away,
Far off from the gates of gold—
Away on the mountains wild and bare,
Away from the tender Shepherd's care.

"Lord, Thou hast here Thy ninety and nine;
Are they not enough for Thee?"
But the Shepherd made answer: "This of mine
Has wandered away from me;
And altho' the road be rough and steep,
I go to the desert to find my sheep."

But none of the ransomed ever knew
How deep were the waters crossed;
Nor how dark was the night that the Lord passed thro'
Ere He found His sheep that was lost.
Out in the desert He heard its cry—
Sick and helpless, and ready to die.

But all thro' the mountains, thunder-riv'n,
And up from the rocky steep,
There arose a glad cry to the gate of heav'n,
"Rejoice! I have found my sheep!"
And the angels echoed around the throne,
"Rejoice, for the Lord brings back His own!"

—ELIZABETH CECILIA CLEPHANE, 1830–1869

$\mathcal{M}$an born of woman is of few days . . .

—JOB 14:1

All I have needed,

Thy hand hath provided;

Great is Thy faithfulness,

Lord, unto me!

Great Is Thy Faithfulness

Chapter 9

AS WE APPROACH THE FALL AND WINTER OF LIFE

Fall has always been a special time of year for me. Oh, I love the newness of spring and the warm lazy days of summer, but fall is special. I love the bright blue of a clear autumn sky. I love the cool days, the trees beginning to look as if their leaves had been touched by a master's paintbrush. The mountains aflame in the late afternoon sun with yellow, red, orange, gold, and bronze . . .

I love to walk through leaves that crunch beneath my feet and breathe fresh, crisp air. I love the cozy feeling of approaching winter. Open fires on the hearth, enticing smells in the kitchen, holidays to prepare for . . . There is something warm and inviting about fall and winter.

As I begin to experience the autumn years of my life, I am discovering that they, too, are special.

After the long, fun-filled, sometimes hectic days during the summer of my life, when my children were growing up, I wondered what would fall be like? Would it be dreary? Depressing? Lonely? Or would I find it as invigorating as a beautiful, crisp autumn day in the mountains of North Carolina or Switzerland? I have found it to be a bit of both.

The autumn years are not always easy. Anne Morrow Lindbergh referred to them as the barnacle years. These are the years when we seem to carry around a lot of extra weight, things that cling to us like barnacles—the concerns of children, grandchildren, elderly parents, financial concerns, menopause, our own aging and health problems, saying good-bye to those we love, the adjustments of an empty nest, and retirement. All of these and many more can make these years ones of concern, anxiety, and worry.

King David was not a stranger to these feelings. I think that one of the reasons he was called a man after God's own heart was his honesty, transparency, and vulnerability before God and others. During one difficult time he says, "I am so troubled that I cannot speak" (Ps. 77:4 KJV). He goes on to wonder if God had forgotten him or cast him off. But then David begins to remember. He begins to allow his mind to think on "these things," as the apostle Paul encourages us to do (Phil 4:8)—to think on all the good things that God had done in his life, all God's gifts and mercies, how God had led him, protected him, comforted him. David says that he would meditate on all these things and then share them with others. This decision not only calmed David's anxieties, but it also has been a source of encouragement to many thousands all these years.

How important it is for us to remember. This not only calms our fears, but strengthens our faith.

A few years ago, I was speeding along the freeway on my way to a dinner engagement. At the moment, I was bathed in the warm glow of the late afternoon sun, but a fierce, black thunderstorm loomed ahead of me. A few miles down the road, large drops of rain began to pelt my car and jagged bolts of lightning lit up the ominous sky. I looked behind me in the rearview mirror and saw the glorious colors of a South Florida sunset over the Everglades. Then looking ahead again, suddenly before me was a perfect, complete rainbow.

I was so filled with emotion that I pulled off of the road just to let my heart meditate on what this meant to me. As I looked again at the sunset behind me, it reminded me of all of His goodness to me in the past—how His love had saved me, how His grace had kept me, how His mercies had surrounded me. I looked again at the rainbow bright against the stormy sky and thought of all of His promises. I thought of His faithfulness in keeping these promises and how He had never failed me. This little incident not only encouraged me, but it gave me courage and strength to face the next storm.[1]

Mother has a sign over her desk that reads, "Fear not tomorrow, God is already there." As we get older, we tend to have concerns about the future. Even if we are not worried, we wonder and question because of the uncertainties.

There is a narrow, winding road that leads through the village in Switzerland where we lived. In order to go down the other side of the mountain, we had to cross a bridge that spans a deep ravine. Until it was repaired and rebuilt a few years ago, it was a bit frightening to cross. It was old, rickety, and narrow. The mountain train shared this same bridge, and if it happened to be coming at the same time our car approached the bridge, it was downright scary. One day as we approached the bridge, our six-year-old expressed fearful concern that it might collapse under the weight of our car. To this his younger sister quickly said, "Stephan, look up, not down; then you won't be scared."

The Scriptures also encourage us to look up. Do you remember after Jesus was buried, three women came to the tomb to anoint his body with spices? They were worried and concerned, and they asked, "Who will roll the stone away from the entrance of the tomb?" The Scriptures tell us, "When they looked up, they saw that the stone, which was very large, had been rolled away" (Mark 16:3–4).

So it is with our lives. So often I am concerned about a present circumstance or something in the future; but when I look up and depend on Him, I discover that it was nothing to be concerned over. The stone was already rolled away. What stone is keeping you concerned?

As I look back on my life, at the various stones that blocked my way, I am reminded of the words to the magnificent hymn, "All I have needed Thy hand has provided." And I know that He will continue to provide all I need.

Paul tells us to press on; these women tell us to look up. Mother is still doing both. There are few I know who have managed to make the most of the time they have left on this side of heaven the way Mother has, yet she feels there is still so much to do, as she expressed in the following poem:

A little more time,
Lord,
just a little more time.
There's so much to do,
so much undone.
If it's all right with You
Lord,

please stop the sun.
There's forever before me
forever with You;
but a little more time
for there's so much to do.

—RUTH BELL GRAHAM

Mother is now in her eighties and, although she still feels there is so much to do, she is in frail health and knows her time here on earth is limited. She has shared with me that her thoughts often return to her childhood home in China, her little attic room, the times of reading and doing handiwork around the living room fire at night, all the happy times with the missionaries in the mission compound.

I am discovering that my autumn years are filled with similar moments. Moments of reflection . . . looking back . . . remembering . . . being introspective. Just as during the fall months of the year, I discover my thoughts, feelings, and activities turning inward, preparing to spend more time beside the fireplace reading, instead of outside in the garden planting and weeding. So it is with my thoughts and my spirit during these fall years of my life.

There are also other moments, moments of wondering "what if." What if I had chosen a different path? What if I had made other choices in my life? What if I had picked another mate? What if I had finished school or chosen a different career or only had two children?

I find that I am spending more time thinking of the past, remembering the innocence and newness of the spring years in the mountains of North Carolina and the happy, sunny days full of energy and activity during the summer years of mothering a large brood. Yes, there are times when my thoughts tumble into a moment of fog—questions about the future and concerns over health or finances, doubts, uncertainties. These moments don't last long, but they are there.

Introspection is an important part of life, but we must be careful not to tumble over the cliff into the quicksand of morbid introspection allowing Satan to discourage us and defeat us in our fall and winter years.

A few weeks ago, a friend gave me a beautiful white orchid plant. A few mornings later, I was sitting on my brick terrace feeding the birds and squirrels. The blue jays strutted and squawked as they competed with the frisky squirrels for the best and the biggest seeds. In the background a woodpecker could be heard insistently working hard for its breakfast, while the gentle morning doves cooed softly, waiting patiently their turn. Lady May, my little dog, would bark every now and then, which caused quite a stir of fluttering and scampering. All the while Simon, our very large tabby cat, silently waited his turn to cause trouble.

While observing this feeding frenzy, I happened to look more closely at the magnificent large, white blossoms of my new orchid. Each detail was magnificent, the soft shades of yellow filling the center surrounded by delicate, deep red markings. I looked at the various birds who had quickly assembled upon seeing me put out the seed. I smiled to myself as I once again thought of the words of Matthew: "Do not worry about your life. . . . Look at the birds of the air; they do not sow or reap or store away in barns, and yet your heavenly Father feeds them. . . . See how the lilies of the field grow [or this lovely orchid]. They do not labor or spin. Yet I tell you that not even Solomon in all his splendor was dressed like one of these" (6:26–9). Matthew goes on to warn us that worrying doesn't add one single moment to our lives. So what is the point? I often think of the words of the hymn we used to sing when I was young:

> Trust and obey
> For there's no other way
> To be happy in Jesus
> But to trust and obey.

Daddy has often been asked what has been the greatest surprise of his life. His answer: "The brevity of it." Yes, life is brief. The Scriptures remind us of this when they tell us that it is like the grass that quickly dries up and is gone. Job said that our days are few and full of trouble (see Job 14:1).

This life is not only brief, but C. S. Lewis reminded us that the death rate in every generation is 100 percent. The most absolute certainty of life is death. This is why it is so important that each one of us has that quiet knowing that this life is only the beginning.

If we know in Whom we believe and we are certain of our relationship with Him, then we do not have to be afraid of death or avoid the subject of death. Although death will be a shadow, an uncertainty with all sorts of questions and doubts surrounding it, I can embrace it with a quiet knowing that He is mine and I am His and He will be with me.

A few years ago, while watching the funerals of Mother Teresa and Princess Di, I was struck by the contrast. Two world-renowned women—one young and glamorous, the other plain, wrinkled, and aged. Both were important to and had greatly influenced the world in which they lived. But the most remarkable difference to me was in the tone of the two funerals—one was magnificent, the other awesome in its utter simplicity.

The distinction was obvious. Princess Di's funeral was lovely and it was obvious that she was well loved, but it was Mother Teresa's funeral that echoed loud and clear

that she was a woman whose life had been blessed with certainties. She had possessed the quiet knowing that all was well between her Lord and her.

My mother-in-law experienced this same quietness the day she passed through the valley of the shadow of death. She was ninety-seven years old, and until a month before her death, she had been in very good health. I was at her bedside most of the day. Her breathing was labored; we knew it wouldn't be long. But she had no fear, no anxiety. She knew she had placed her trust in Him many years before. She had that quiet knowing, and He gave her a peace that He would not fail her. And He will not fail you or me.

I think if Mother had to pick one favorite hymn for this time of her life, it would be "Great Is Thy Faithfulness." Mother has had a very rich, full, rewarding life. Being born in China of missionary parents, going to high school in North Korea, meeting Daddy (never realizing the challenges that lay ahead as his wife), having children, friends, travel, writing projects, her poetry. All of these things have meant so much to her. And many of those whom she loves have gone on ahead. As she expresses in the following poem, she realizes that she not only has a full life of happy memories, but she also has a lot to look forward to:

And when I die
I hope my soul ascends
slowly, so that I
may watch the earth receding
out of sight,
its vastness growing smaller
as I rise,
savoring its recession
with delight.
Anticipating joy
is itself a joy.
And joy unspeakable
and full of glory

needs more
than "in the twinkling of an eye,"
more than "in a moment."

Lord, who am I to disagree?
It's only we
have much to leave behind;
so much . . . Before.
These moments
of transition
will, for me, be
time
to adore.

—Ruth Bell Graham

As I read this poem, it is difficult not to become very emotional. She's not only my mother; she's my best friend, and it's going to be very difficult to say good-bye to her. But my loss will be heaven's gain. It is at times like this that I realize anew the importance of a quiet knowing, that assurance that I will see my friend again.

Quickly the circles are going around. It seems like just yesterday that I was playing in the little stream that bounced over the mica-encrusted rocks beside our home. Soon I would hear my grandfather's car as he turned up the steep grade on Louisiana Road. He would honk and I would run up the drive, through the little gray gate, and across the road to his house. Now my grandchildren are playing in the same stream, and I'm a grandmother living across the street.

As I get older and my death and the death, of my parents get nearer, I think more about heaven. In fact, the more loved ones who go before me make heaven all the more enticing and cozy—more like "home."

While writing this chapter, I asked Mother what it feels like growing old. Her quick, witty reply was, "I don't like the aches and pains of growing old, but when I was young I had cramps every month, too. And I didn't enjoy those either."

I then asked what her favorite part of growing old is. Without hesitation she replied, "The memories . . . all the happy memories."

My friend Edith Schaeffer has said that she expects in heaven for us to have our same personalities, tics, and idiosyncrasies, only perfected. Knowing Mother, I have to chuckle. Heaven will never be the same. I love her wit and her spunk as well as her wisdom and winsomeness. And I surely will miss her when she's gone. But knowing that she is already there will make me look forward to going, too.

In her old age and even as she approaches death, Mother continues to be an example to me. It's like watching a magnificent sunset. I watch enthralled, wishing it to last forever, hoping that it will take its time before dipping into the sea or dropping behind the mountain peak. Then it does, and for a long time afterward, I sit still, basking in its afterglow, so thankful that I was privileged to share in its awesome beauty. So it will be with Mother.

Mother has always considered life as a work in progress. When she dies, she wants her epitaph to read, "End of construction. Thank you for your patience."

Great Is Thy Faithfulness

Great is Thy faithfulness, O God, my Father,
There is no shadow of turning with Thee;
Thou changest not, Thy compassions, they fail not;
As Thou hast been, Thou forever wilt be.

REFRAIN:
Great is Thy faithfulness!
Great is Thy faithfulness!
Morning by morning new mercies I see;
All I have needed, Thy hand hath provided;
Great is Thy faithfulness, Lord, unto me!

Summer and winter, and springtime and harvest,
Sun, moon, and stars in their courses above
Join with all nature in manifold witness
To Thy great faithfulness, mercy, and love.

(Refrain)

Pardon for sin and a peace that endureth,
Thine own dear presence to cheer and to guide;
Strength for today and bright hope for tomorrow,
Blessings all mine, with ten thousand beside!

(Refrain)

WORDS: THOMAS O. CHISHOLM, 1866–1960; COPYRIGHT © 1923, 1951
BY HOPE PUBLISHING COMPANY. 380 SOUTH MAIN PLACE, CAROL
STREAM, IL 60188. (800-323-1049) ALL RIGHTS RESERVED.
USED BY PERMISSION.

The glory of young men
is their strength,
gray hair the splendor
of the old.

—Proverbs 20:29 (NIV)

C h a p t e r

10

Even This

FINDING BLESSINGS IN OUR BURDENS

One of my favorite saints is a feisty nun who lived in the 1500s. She was once quoted as saying, "Lord, no wonder you have so few friends if you treat them all like you treat me."

We may chuckle, but I bet you, too, have felt like this at times. Have you ever been disappointed with God? Maybe when the burdens of life are just too great and the storms of life have left you so battered and bruised that you just don't have the strength to go on?

No one is exempt from burdens. We all carry some kind of burden, heartache, guilt, or concern. And I think that especially women in our present culture are often asked to carry burdens that the Lord never intended for them to carry. Many are carrying burdens that they have little or no control over. An unloving husband, a wayward child, the loss of a job, or health concerns. We cry out with Job, "My heart is in turmoil" (30:27 NKJV), "My soul is weary" (10:1 KJV), "Where then is my hope?" (17:15). We cry out with Moses, "The burden is too great for me. I cannot carry it alone" (see Exod. 18:18; Deut. 1:9, 12; Num. 11:13).

A few years ago we purchased a sailboat. We had never owned a boat or sailed before, and we knew nothing about either. However, we thought that it would be a nice family experience, so we took the plunge (no pun intended) and bought the boat. I became quite interested in the different aspects of sailing. One intriguing aspect was that much of the value of the sailboat lay in the amount of lead it carried in its keel. The weight was significant for it was the stabilizing factor for the craft. It gave balance.

The builders knew just how much weight the boat could safely and effectively handle. Too much weight and it would move laboriously through the water; too little weight and it would be unable to maintain the necessary depth and begin to reel dangerously from side to side.

This boat also carried another vital weight—the

anchor. When we found ourselves in unfamiliar water or too far out to sea without the necessary experience or near anything solid to which we could secure our boat, we would just drop anchor. The boat would turn and sway, pull and tug, but it remained safe because of the weight of its keel and the anchor that held it in place.

These weights were essential. But only an experienced master builder knows exactly how much and where to place the weight.

Weights or burdens are also important in our lives. We all need moorings, things that give balance and depth to our lives, things that keep us steady, on course, moving in the right direction, anchored to Him.

Burdens keep us aware of our need of Him. David said, "In my distress I called to the Lord" (see 2 Sam. 22:7; Ps. 18:6; 118:5; 120:1 NIV). How often in my own experience, when things are going well, I forget to depend on the Lord. I don't even feel the same need to call upon Him or to abide in His Word. But when the storms come and the troubles arise, I am drawn right back to the Anchor.

God did not send Jesus into the world to remove all burdens and heartache, nor even to explain them. But He sent Jesus to be with us in and through them.

Do you remember the story of the three men in the fiery furnace? They knew that God could deliver them and they had faith that He would, but I love their attitude when they said to the king, "Our God whom we serve is able to deliver us from the burning fiery furnace, and he will deliver us out of thine hand, O king, But if not, be it known unto thee, O king, that we will not serve thy gods, nor worship the golden image which thou hast set up" (Dan. 3:17–18 KJV).

Some years ago in England, one evening just after dusk, a small boy was watching the lamplighter as he lit the street lamps one after another. His mother called him to come to bed. When he didn't respond, she went to look for him. "What are you doing?" she asked when she found him. "I am watching the man put holes in the darkness," the small boy answered.

A QUIET KNOWING

This is what Jesus does for us. He doesn't take away all the darkness, but He puts holes in it. . . . He lights it up with Himself.

Burdens are also important because they draw us to one another. We do not have to carry our burdens alone. The Scriptures tell us to "Bear one another's burdens, and so fulfill the law of Christ" (Gal. 6:2 NKJV). What did God do for Moses when he cried out that the burden was too heavy? He sent him seventy able men to help him.

When my prodigal son ran away from home, I sat down on a bench down by the lake on our property. I was so devastated, hurt, concerned, anxious, and worried. I sat there for some time praying and talking to the Lord. I asked the Lord to reveal Himself in a special way to me so that I could know that His presence was there with me. I sat waiting. I didn't feel anything or see anything special, just heaviness. As it got dark and the lights in the other

houses around the lake began to turn out, I asked again, "Lord, it's dark now, and it's just You and me. No one else will see it, so could you please reveal Yourself to me by letting me see an angel?"

I happen to believe that God can do anything He wants, and I believe in angels. I also knew that if He wanted to He could very well let me see one. I waited some more. Nothing. "Lord," I pleaded again, "if You won't show me an angel, could You at least let one flick his wing over against that dark pine tree? . . . Please?"

I waited some more. Nothing. Finally, I went back to the house and with a heavy heart crawled into bed without having any special sense of His presence. Only heaviness.

The next morning, I got up and somehow got the other children all off to school and the house picked up. Suddenly the phone rang. It was our pastor. "Gigi, we just heard about Tullian and we will be there shortly to pray with you." Again the phone. "Gigi," the voice of a dear friend said, "We are on our way, and don't worry about dinner." Again the phone. "Gigi, I am closing down the office and taking my staff down to the beach to look for Tullian," the voice of our insurance agent said. All day long the phone rang. That night when I went to bed, I said, "Thank You, Lord, for revealing Yourself to me in such a special way, not by seeing an angel, but through other believers . . . the body."

This is what the Christian life is all about—serving one another, bearing one another's burdens. But in order to take advantage of this blessing, we need three things.

First, we need to be vulnerable. We need to be able to admit that we have a burden. Now I don't mean being indiscriminate, telling everyone we meet our problems, but we need someone, or maybe our small Bible study group, or a special friend or prayer partner to whom we can go, pour out our hearts to, and pray with.

Second, those of us who are not at this moment carrying a burden need to be available. If we are too busy, too committed, and too overwhelmed with our own concerns, then we can't be available to help carry the burdens of others.

Third, we have to be approachable. I know many Christians, including pastor's wives and Christian leaders, to whom I would never go with a problem or burden. They are simply not approachable.

I once sat across the aisle on a plane from a man who was reading. This man was very uptight and stiff. But, since I am always curious as to what people are reading, I looked over and to my surprise he was reading a book entitled *How to Win Souls*. Soon, his seatmate approached, tried to smile, and sat down without the slightest bit of acknowledgment from this stiff, uptight Christian. He never did smile, never said hello or "How are you?" . . . nothing, not even a farewell. I thought to myself, *Well, good luck, buddy, trying to win souls.*

We have to be approachable, friendly, warm, and caring. And we must often keep our mouths shut. Those who are heavily burdened don't need Bible verses shouted at them; they probably know them all by heart anyway. What they need is a sympathetic ear, a loving arm around their shoulders, and maybe some practical help.

Do you remember the story of Elijah after his great victory on Mount Carmel? (see 1 Kings 19). He had incurred the wrath of the very wicked and very powerful queen. He had killed all of her prophets, so she sent her forces out to kill Elijah. The Scriptures tell us that Elijah was afraid and ran for his life. In fact, he ran more than one hundred miles, left his servant there, and continued on another day's journey into the wilderness. There he sat down under a little low broom tree and said, "Lord I have had enough; take my life." He wanted to die. Then, exhausted, Elijah fell asleep.

Have you been there? Have you ever been so discouraged and depressed that you wanted to die? Maybe you have even attempted to end your life or, if not, have wished for God to end it.

Elijah was physically tired, emotionally worn out, and spiritually exhausted. So often it is after a great victory that Satan causes us to become discouraged and oppressed.

How did God react to Elijah? He didn't berate him or say how disappointed He was in him. He didn't tell him how ashamed He was of him after all He had done for him and all the victories He had given him. He didn't even preach to him a three-pointed, alliterated sermon on "Thou shalt not be depressed."

Instead, He sent an angel to fix him a good meal, to care for his needs. After Elijah had eaten, he fell asleep again. After a good night of rest, the Lord sent the angel again to fix another good meal and Elijah was strengthened.

How tender our God is. How understanding, how patient, how caring.

The apostle Peter encourages us to "cast all your anxiety on him, because he cares for you" (1 Pet. 5:7). Jesus Himself invites all who are carrying heavy burdens to come to Him, and He promises to give them rest (see Matt. 11:28).

There is no mention of the size or shape of the burden. No problem is too small or insignificant and no burden to big or load too heavy. He knows us and how much weight we can carry. He is the Master Builder.

The Scriptures tell us that He knows us by name (see Exod. 33:12), that the very hairs of our head are numbered (see Matt. 10:30), and that He not only sees our tears, but He cares so much that He gathers them and puts them in a bottle (see Ps. 56:8 KJV).

This is the God Who walks with us and helps us carry our heavy loads. He knows our frames, our makeup, and our limitations. He remembers that we are frail, and He has promised not to give us more than we can take. This is the quiet knowing that we have as we carry our individual burdens through life.

When Peter's mother-in-law was sick, Jesus took her by the hand and "lifted her up" (Mark 1:31 KJV).

When David was fleeing from his own son who was trying to kill him, he said, "Thou, O LORD, art a shield for me; . . . and the lifter up of mine head" (Ps. 3:3 KJV).

When Job was in the midst of his suffering and sorrow, his friends reminded him, "When men are cast down . . . there is lifting up" (Job 22:29 KJV).

When Peter's faith failed and he began to sink, the Lord took him by the hand and lifted him into the boat (see Matt. 14:30–31).

When we are burdened and feel overwhelmed . . . about to sink beneath the load, we must focus our faith on Him and not on our circumstances. Yes, there is a lifting up. The nail-pierced hands of Jesus reach out to us and lift us up when we need it. There are blessings in burdens.

It is the difficulties, the weights of life, that cause us to depend on Him. They are often the very thing that keeps us anchored to Him. Paul, James, and Peter all tell us that it is the trials and burdens of life that are used to deepen, mature, and complete our faith (see Rom. 5:3–5; James 1:2–4; 1 Pet. 1:6–7).

Remember the Swiss mountains? It is not on the mountaintops where the fruit is grown, but in the fog-filled valleys. As the old Arab proverb says, "All sunshine makes a desert." Our burdens, heartaches, and painful experiences can be used to help and encourage others.

Tucked into the story of the feeding of the five thousand, there is a wonderful little verse that often goes unnoticed. "When they had all had enough to eat, he said to his disciples, 'Gather the pieces that are left over. Let nothing be wasted'" (John 6:12).

If God doesn't waste the fragments of bread, do you think He would waste the fragments of our lives? God does not waste anything—not our experiences, not our tears, not our heartaches, not our sorrows, nothing. If given to Him, He will gather the fragments.

What burden are you carrying today? Jesus says, "Come to Me." Remember, "When he giveth quietness, who then can make trouble?" (Job 34:29 KJV).

This is the quiet knowing that He offers.

For God so loved the world
that he gave his one and only Son,
that whoever believes in him
shall not perish but have eternal life.

—JOHN 3:16

Softly and tenderly Jesus is calling,

Calling for you and for me;

Come home, come home,

Ye who are weary come home;

Earnestly, tenderly, Jesus is calling,

Calling, O sinner, come home!

Softly and Tenderly, Jesus Is Calling

THE PREREQUISITE FOR A QUIET KNOWING

At an early age, I answered this calling.

One day, when I was four years old, I woke up sick. Instead of bounding out of bed to play, I stayed all day in my bedroom right next to my parents' room. There was a special cupboard in my room, up high out of my reach, where a few toys, books, and dolls were kept for just such days.

Mother would come in and out of my room to see how I was, read me a book, or bring me a glass of something cool to drink. On one of these trips, she reached up, opened the little cupboard, and took one of these "treasures" out for me. It helped to make being sick almost fun.

Later in the afternoon, when things were quieter, she

came and sat down on my bed. We talked about lots of things. Then, I am not sure how, we got on the subject of my "badness." It was not hard for me to understand that I was bad, because as a feisty, spunky, rambunctious four-year-old with a mind of my own, I was bad and was told this fact often. In fact, Mother will confirm that I was spanked pretty regularly.

Some people feel that being born into a Christian family automatically makes you a Christian. But God doesn't have grandchildren. Yes, being part of a Christian family did give me the advantage of being introduced to Him early, but it didn't make me a Christian. Others think that being baptized at an early age, going regularly to church, or going through the rituals of confirmation makes you a Christian. But none of these things do. They

can't. It is only by the grace of God that we are saved. Only a personal encounter with God through Jesus Christ makes one a Christian.

Sitting on my bed that day long ago, Mother pointed out to me that I couldn't go to heaven when I died with all my badness and that the only Person Who could take this badness away was Jesus. She explained that God loved me so very much that He had sent His only Son, Jesus, to die on a cross in order to take the punishment for all my badness. She quoted John 3:16 to me, putting in my name: "For God so loved Gigi that He gave His one and only Son, that if Gigi believed in Him she shall not perish, but have eternal life." She then asked me if I'd like to ask Jesus into my heart to take away my badness. Of course, I wanted Jesus in my heart. So I simply bowed my head and opened my heart to Him that day. I didn't understand all the theological implications of my decision; I was just a little girl. But my salvation was real.

There is a story told about Karl Barth, the great Swiss theologian, who was lecturing in one of Switzerland's prestigious seminaries. One of the students asked him, "Dr. Barth, what is the greatest theological truth that you have learned?" Dr. Barth answered, "The greatest theological truth that I have learned, is 'Jesus loves me, this I know, for the Bible tells me so.'" That is a theology we can all understand at any age.

But it doesn't end there. Scripture tells us that when God begins a good work in our lives, He will continue to perform it (see Phil. 1:6). I will be forever grateful that I came to know Him at such an early age, but I am also very aware that He has and will continue to work in my life.

Mother says the best way to make children eat their dinner is for them to see you thoroughly enjoying yours. I grew up in a community where the men and women led the kind of lives that I wanted. They gave me an appetite for what they had because they thoroughly enjoyed their faith. It was a vital part of their everyday lives. They were fun-loving, balanced, and deeply committed to Jesus Christ. And I wanted to be like them.

I find today that so many Christians are not appetizing. We are not making the people around us, including our children, hungry for what we have.

Mother tells me that one morning when we were small, she awoke after a bad night's sleep to discover that she had overslept. Without even combing her hair or pausing for makeup, she hurriedly pulled on her robe, lifted Franklin out of his crib without bothering to change his diaper, and set him in the highchair. She proceeded to set the table hurriedly for breakfast so that we would not be late for school. That morning, every time I opened my mouth to say something, Bunny interrupted. Finally, in exasperation, I slammed down my fork. "Mother!" I exclaimed. "Between listening to Bunny and smelling Franklin and looking at you, I'm just not hungry!"

This is true of many Christians. Between looking at some of us, smelling the attitudes of others of us, and listening to others of us, they are not hungry for what we have.

Although I want to be like those Christians around whom I grew up, I have failed so often and am often concerned that my life as a Christian is not always appetizing. But there is grace. God's grace is greater than all my sin; it is truly amazing grace.

I heard the story of an old Italian artist who had lost some of his skill. One evening he sat discouraged before a painting he had just completed. He noticed that he had lost some of his touch. The canvas didn't burst with life as his previous work had once done. As he went to bed, his son heard him say, "I have failed, I have failed."

Later that evening, his son, also an artist, came to examine his father's work, and he, too, noticed that it did not reflect his father's usual work. Taking the palette and brush, he worked far into the night, adding a little touch here, a smudge there, a little color here, a bit of depth, a shadow or two, some highlights. The son worked until he knew that the work would fulfill his father's vision.

Morning came, and the father descended into the studio. He stood before the perfect canvas and in utter delight exclaimed, "Why, I have wrought better than I knew!"

We, too, like this painting, fall short of the Father's glory. Scripture tells us, "All have sinned and fall short of the glory of God" (Rom. 3:23). And although we may try through good works, church attendance, or charitable deeds, it is impossible to restore ourselves.

But the Son, Jesus, came and gave His life on the cross so that He could restore us. If we give Him the canvas of our lives, He will begin the restoration process. He will touch up here and there, add a bit of depth, some color and highlights, and even a shadow or two. Each canvas will receive His personal attention, His unique strokes,

His finishing touches. He will work until the canvas reflects the Father's glory. Then, when it is complete, the Scriptures tell us that He will present us faultless before His Father in heaven (see Jude 1:24). On that day, we, too, because of Jesus, will be able to exclaim with utter joy, "Oh, I did better than I thought!"

Jesus is the Quiet Knowing. Softly and tenderly, He is calling each of us. He speaks in a quiet, gentle voice (see 1 Kings 19:12). He tells us that He stands at the door and knocks, and He will come in for whoever opens the door (see Rev. 3:20). He is a gentleman and will never force us to answer His call.

Is He calling you? Is He knocking at the door of your heart and life? His soft and tender calling, and your response to it, is the beginning of A Quiet Knowing.

SOFTLY AND TENDERLY

Softly and tenderly Jesus is calling,
Calling for you and for me;
See, on the portals He's waiting and watching,
Watching for you and for me.

REFRAIN:
Come home, come home,
Ye who are weary come home;
Earnestly, tenderly, Jesus is calling,
Calling, O sinner, come home!

Why should we tarry when Jesus is pleading,
Pleading for you and for me?
Why should we linger and heed not His mercies,
Mercies for you and for me?
(Refrain)

Time is now fleeting, the moments are passing,
Passing from you and from me;
Shadows are gathering, deathbeds are coming,
Coming for you and for me.
(Refrain)

Oh! for the wonderful love He has promised,
Promised for you and for me;
Tho' we have sinned He has mercy and pardon,
Pardon for you and for me.
(Refrain)

WORDS: WILL L. THOMPSON, 1847–1909.

Notes

INTRODUCTION

1. William Barclay, "Philippians," *Daily Study Bible: New Testament* (Philadelphia: Westminster Press, 1993).

CHAPTER 2

1. Geoffrey Bles, ed., *George MacDonald Anthology* (n.p.: n.d.).
2. Oswald Chambers, *My Utmost for His Highest*, (Grand Rapids, Mich.: Discovery House, 1992), May 26.

CHAPTER 3

1. Source unknown.

CHAPTER 4

1. "In the Garden," words by C. Austin Miles, 1868–1946.

CHAPTER 9

1. Adapted from *Currents of the Heart* by Gigi Graham Tchividjian, (Multnomah Press, Portland, Oregon, copyright © 1996). Used with permission.

The following poems are taken from Ruth Bell Graham's *Collected Poems*, copyright © 1977, 1992, 1997, 1998, published by Baker Book House Company. Used by permission.
"Sunk in this gray depression I cannot pray"
"'Give me your nights,' the quiet voice of God said"
"Into the heart of the Infinite"
"Your eyes look down at me"
"If I could have each day one hour of sun"
"Those splendid, soaring jagged peaks"
"The hills on which I need to gaze"
"Above the clouds thick, boiling, low"
"I met you years ago"
"God, bless all young mothers at the end of day"
"Like other shepherds help me keep watch"

Don't miss "A Quiet Knowing — Canticles For The Heart" featuring the favorite hymns of Ruth Bell Graham. The CD features twelve instrumental renditions of ten traditional and two contemporary hymns containing strong Celtic and Appalachian influences. Songs include: *Softly and Tenderly Jesus Is Calling* • *A Quiet Knowing* • *Amazing Grace* • *Great Is Thy Faithfulness* • *Just As I Am* • *The Ninety and Nine* • *Be Thou My Vision* • *Children of the Heavenly Father* • *Jesus Loves Me* • *Love Divine* • *Come Ye Sinners* • *Even If*

A QUIET KNOWING—CANTICLES FOR THE HEART
Jeff Johnson & Brian Dunning with John Fitzpatrick
AKD-1504 www.arkmusic.com
Toll free ordering: 877-733-8820